GOD AND MAN
IN THE OLD TESTAMENT

GOD AND MAN
IN THE
OLD TESTAMENT

by

J. A. WAINWRIGHT

*Education Secretary, British Council of Churches
Formerly Senior Lecturer in Religious Education
Saint Paul's College, Cheltenham*

LONDON
NATIONAL SOCIETY
S·P·C·K
1962

*First published in 1962
by The National Society and S.P.C.K.
Holy Trinity Church
Marylebone Road
London N.W.1*

*Printed in Great Britain by
The Talbot Press (S.P.C.K.)
Saffron Walden, Essex*

© J. A. Wainwright, 1962

CONTENTS

Introduction		vii
1. Exodus Faith and Covenant People		1
2. The Nature of God		13
	The Unity of God	13
	The Love and Mercy of God	17
	The Justice of God	23
	The Holiness of God	29
	God the Saviour and Redeemer	32
	God the King	44
	God the Judge	49
	The God of History	53
	The God of Nature and Creation	55
	"To whom then will you liken God?"	65
3. The Nature of Man		76
	Man and his make-up	76
	Man and society	87
	DETACHED NOTE "Israel" and the Racial Unity of the Hebrews	92
	Man, sin, and suffering	93
	DETACHED NOTE The Doctrine of Original Sin	103
	The Destiny of Man	107
	Life after Death	109
4. The Relations between God and Man		113
	Prophecy and the Prophets	113

CONTENTS

DETACHED NOTE
Prophecy and the Cultus 119
The Torah 122
Personal Religion 123
The Spirit of God 128
Worship, Sacrifice, and Priesthood 132

EPILOGUE 161

FOR FURTHER STUDY 163

INDEX OF BIBICAL REFERENCES 166

INTRODUCTION

It is a sound educational principle that experience must always precede understanding. One of the difficulties of understanding the Old Testament is that the experiences of the people for whom it was originally written were very different from ours, and if we try to interpret it in terms of our modern Western European experience, we shall be led sadly astray. One of the essential preliminaries of fruitful Bible study, therefore, is to soak oneself in the thought of the Bible, so that it is possible to read it with the eyes and understanding of the men for whom it was intended. This is particularly the case since the Bible was not written in English, and any translation, however good, can only begin to convey the full meaning of the original. Words are the means by which ideas are communicated, and to understand words is to make a good start in understanding the ideas expressed also.

This little book is an attempt to introduce those who have some knowledge of Old Testament *history* to Old Testament *ideas*. Inevitably a large part of it is taken up with the study of word meanings. It is hoped that this will not prove a dull exercise to be skipped, but what it has been to the author, a thrilling voyage of discovery. It has been written especially for the use of teachers: for no one can hope to communicate the meaning of the Bible till he has understood it himself. It is highly improbable that it will provide ready-made lesson material, but by helping the teacher to think more deeply about his material should lead to a better understanding on the part of the taught.

It must be emphasized that this is not a complete survey of the subject. That would take a very much larger book than this. Its function is simply to act as a stimulus and starting point for further study : if it has done this, it will have succeeded.

Biblical quotations all through are taken from the Revised Standard Version of the Bible, copyright 1946 and 1952, by permission of Thomas Nelson and Sons, Ltd.

The substance of this book was originally given as lectures to the Supplementary Course in Religious Education at St Paul's College, Cheltenham, in 1959-60 and 1960-61. To those who suffered it then, and made many helpful suggestions and criticisms, my thanks are more than due. I must acknowledge also the help and encouragement I have received from the Reverend Professor A. S. Herbert, B.D., of Selly Oak Colleges, Birmingham (how much of this book is really his is a mystery), from Professor D. Winton Thomas, M.A., Regius Professor of Hebrew in the University of Cambridge, who read the book in manuscript and made many most helpful suggestions; and from my colleague Mr P. R. Epps, who has saved me from many solecisms in expression.

Cheltenham,   J.A.W.
September 1961

CHAPTER ONE

EXODUS FAITH AND COVENANT PEOPLE

> For you are a people holy to the LORD your God; the LORD your God has chosen you to be a people for his own possession, out of all the peoples that are on the face of the earth. It was not because you were more in number than any other people that the LORD set his love upon you and chose you, for you were the fewest of all peoples; but it is because the LORD loves you, and is keeping the oath which he swore to your fathers, that the LORD has brought you out with a mighty hand, and redeemed you from the house of bondage, from the hand of Pharaoh king of Egypt. Know therefore that the LORD your God is God, the faithful God who keeps covenant and steadfast love with those who love him and keep his commandments, to a thousand generations. (Deut. 7. 6-9)

It is not to much to say that the whole faith of Israel from the time of Moses to the present day depends on the events which we know as the Exodus and the making of the Covenant on Mount Sinai. Israel believed in a God who had once saved them "out of the land of Egypt, out of the house of bondage" with a "mighty hand and an outstretched arm." He had done this because, for some reason known only to himself, he had chosen Israel as a special nation, with a destiny that only they could fulfil. He had bound himself to them by a covenant, which he would keep, and which demanded that they for their part would obey him. This was God's purpose, and nothing that man could do would be allowed to thwart it. What God had done once he could, and would, do again. So, in the darkest times of trouble and danger, Israel remained steadfast in the faith of the God who acts in history, and is in control of the affairs of men and of nations.

The story of the Exodus has been handed down in Hebrew tradition in several different forms, and each of these traditions had been subject to many years of oral tradition before being written in its present form. In this process the story of an event which had such importance for the life of the nation, and in which the hand of God was so clearly seen, was certain to be embroidered and exaggerated so as to heighten the miraculous and emphasize the greatness of the event. When we see discrepancies in the stories, or realize the improbabilities in the narratives, we shall not be surprised. We shall, however, realize that it is extremely difficult to get back to the facts about what really did happen and to reconstruct the events. This does not mean that we can be uncertain of the foundation of these stories. Something did happen: it is woven right into the very fabric of every tradition that we have, even the very earliest, and the picture presented is one that could not have been invented. If we had a story of the way in which the nation had sprung from some mighty hero, or from the union of some god or other with a human woman, we could have added it to the list of hundreds of similar legends. (Traces of such a story are preserved in Gen. 6. 1-4.) If we read of a tribe sprung from the legitimate but dispossessed rulers of a great nation, we could have understood it. Instead, what we have is the story of a gang of slaves, escaped from their masters, with no value or merit of their own, owing their deliverance to a God who had given them everything they had and whom they had disobeyed as soon as they had the chance. Such a story could not have been invented. To exist

EXODUS FAITH AND COVENANT PEOPLE 3

at all, it must have a strong foundation of fact, though this is, of course, far from saying that we can accept at once all the details given in the Pentateuch. Even if we remove the obvious exaggerations, discrepancies in the traditions make it impossible to be sure of exact facts, and any reconstruction can be only tentative. It seems possible, however, that these events took place some time during the fourteenth century B.C. Those concerned were semitic slaves, drawn from the poorest part of those left in Egypt after the expulsion of the (semitic) Hyksos dynasty by Ahmose I about 1580 B.C. All told, there were probably no more than two or three thousand. Having, naturally, been refused permission to leave Egypt and rejoin their kinsmen in Palestine, they took advantage of the confusion caused by a series of natural disasters to escape towards Palestine. They were pursued by a squadron of chariotry, which was held up and partly destroyed in the swamps and shallows of the Gulf of Akaba, while the slaves got away into the desert, into Midianite country east of the Gulf. Their leader was a strong character called Moses, who believed that these events had not happened by accident, but had been brought about by a God called Yahweh, who had given him a special commission to lead these people out of Egypt. They were to meet this God at his holy mountain, and it was there that Moses was the instrument in making the Covenant between Yahweh and the people. It is extremely doubtful if more than a tiny minority had any realization of the significance of what had happened. Yet these events were the birth of a faith which is to-day still one of the great world religions, and which has been father to two others, just as great, Islam and Christianity. These events were the seed from which all later belief and thought sprang, without which the Israelites would have been assimilated without trace into the network of interrelated semitic tribes inhabiting Palestine at the time. Although the story sounds so unpromising, it is hardly possible to doubt that these events were used by God as a means of revealing himself : because the Israelites had this for the foundation of their faith, he could build on it, for in it they had a real glimpse of his nature, very different from the ideas of the nations round about. As we shall see, it is in the events of the Exodus that we can see the beginnings of that theology which controls both the Old and the New Testaments.

We quoted at the head of this chapter a passage from the seventh-century book of Deuteronomy, and anyone who reads that book will find similar passages in abundance. But the Exodus faith is not confined to Deuteronomy: it is the foundation of the work of the prophets :

> When Israel was a child, I loved him, and out of Egypt I called my son. (Hos. 11. 1)

> I am the LORD your God
>   from the land of Egypt;
> you know no God but me,
> and besides me there is no saviour. (Hos. 13. 4)

> Hear this word that the LORD has spoken against you, O people of Israel, against the whole family which I brought up out of the land of Egypt: (Amos 3. 1)

> Thus saith the LORD,
>   who makes a way in the sea,
>   a path in the mighty waters. (Isa. 43. 16)

> What wrong did your fathers find in me
>   that they went far from me,
>   and went after worthlessness, and became worthless?
> They did not say, "Where is the LORD
>   who brought us up from the land of Egypt . . .?"
> (Jer. 2. 5, 6)

> Son of man, there were two women, the daughters of one mother; they played the harlot in Egypt . . . They became mine, and they bore sons and daughters. As for their names . . . Samaria . . . Jerusalem. (Ezek. 23. 2-4)

> As in the days when you came out of the land of Egypt
> I will show them marvellous things. (Mic. 7. 15)

And so on. But the prophets do not merely look *back* to the Exodus: they also look forward to the time when Yahweh, who has once saved his people, will do so again, and they see this salvation as a second Exodus:

> Therefore, behold, the days are coming, says the LORD, when men shall no longer say, "As the LORD lives who brought up the people of Israel out of the land of Egypt," but "As the LORD lives who brought up and led the descendants of the house of Israel out of the north country and out of all the countries where he had driven them . . ." (Jer. 23. 7, 8)

> Awake, awake, put on strength,
> O arm of the LORD;
> awake, as in days of old,
> the generations of long ago.
> Was it not thou that didst cut Rahab in pieces,
> that didst pierce the dragon?
> Was it not thou that didst dry up the sea,
> the waters of the great deep;
> that didst make the depths of the sea a way
> for the redeemed to pass over?
> And the ransomed of the LORD shall return,
> and come with singing to Zion;
> everlasting joy shall be upon their heads;
> they shall obtain joy and gladness,
> and sorrow and sighing shall flee away. (Isa. 51. 9-11)

Examples could be multiplied.

Again, the Ten Words, the foundation of Israelite morality and the basis of the Covenant, begin with God at work in the Exodus:

> I am the LORD your God, who brought you out of the land of Egypt, out of the house of bondage. (Ex. 20. 2; Deut. 5. 6)

In Deuteronomy, obedience to the Law is closely linked with the Exodus:

When your son asks you in time to come, "What is the meaning of the testimonies and the statutes and the ordinances which the Lord our God has commanded you?" then you shall say to your son, "We were Pharaoh's slaves in Egypt; and the Lord brought us out of Egypt with a mighty hand; and the Lord showed signs and wonders, great and grievous, against Egypt and against Pharaoh and all his household, before our eyes; and he brought us out from there, that he might bring us in and give us the land which he swore to give to our fathers. And the Lord commanded us to do all these statutes, to fear the Lord our God, for our good always, that he might preserve us alive, as at this day. (Deut. 6. 20-4)

We should expect to find this foundation belief of Israel emphasized most strongly in worship. Just as the story of the Resurrection of Jesus is found referred to time and again in Christian hymns, so also we find the Exodus story in the Jewish Hymnal, the Psalter. In fact a greater proportion of the Psalms refer to the Exodus than of *Hymns Ancient and Modern* refer to the Resurrection! Two examples of many will suffice:

Our fathers, when they were in Egypt,
    did not consider thy wonderful works;
they did not remember the abundance of thy steadfast love,
    but rebelled against the Most High at the Red Sea.
Yet he saved them for his name's sake,
    that he might make known his mighty power.
He rebuked the Red Sea, and it became dry;
    and he led them through the deep as through a desert.
So he saved them from the hand of the foe,
    and delivered them from the power of the enemy.
And the waters covered their adversaries;
    not one of them was left. (Ps. 106. 7-11)

For it is a statute for Israel,
    an ordinance of the God of Jacob.
He made it a decree in Joseph,
    when he went over the land of Egypt.
I hear a voice I had not known:

"I relieved your shoulder of the burden;
your hands were freed from the basket.
In distress you called, and I delivered you . . .
I am the LORD your God,
who brought you up out of the land of Egypt."

(Ps. 81. 4-7, 10)

The Exodus is found in the very earliest stratum of the Old Testament:

Sing to the LORD, for he has triumphed gloriously;
the horse and his rider he has thrown into the sea.

(Ex. 15. 21)

and it is still part of Jewish ritual to-day. In every Orthodox Jewish household, at the *seder* supper which forms part of Passover celebrations, the youngest present is expected to ask the oldest a series of set questions, to which set answers are given. One of the questions is "Why is this night different from all other nights . . . ?" In reply, the story is retold of the way in which God brought his people out of Egypt to be his peculiar treasure (cf. Ex. 12. 26, 27). In such a way the story must have been handed down for centuries before it was written in the form in which we have it, and a glance through the Jewish *Authorised Daily Prayer Book* will show how deeply it is engrained in Jewish faith to-day.

The Exodus faith is faith in a God who acts, held by a nation who know that they were unable to help themselves then and are still dependent on him. What is the relationship between this God and Israel? In the Old Testament it is seen in terms of *Covenant*. This is a much misunderstood word. It is often thought of as an agreement between God and the nation, or even as a bargain in which the two sides come together and exchange obligations. It cannot be stressed too strongly that this is quite false to the Biblical idea. In the covenant it is always God who is first, who takes the initiative, who dictates the terms of the covenant, and who keeps the covenant. It is the part of Israel to accept what is offered, and to live in accordance with its terms. This will come out more clearly if we look at the usage of the word in the Old Testament.

The Hebrew word is *berith,* and it is used not only of the Divine Covenant, but also of similar relationships between men. The essence of covenant relationship is that both parties are bound together in a community with a common will. This unity is emphasized by the way in which a Covenant was made. We have three accounts of covenant-making in the Old Testament (Gen. 15; Ex. 24. 1-8; Jer. 34. 18, 19). The details differ, but in essence the covenant is made by sharing a sacrificial animal or its blood, the parties to the covenant being bound symbolically between the parts. On the other hand, there is no reason to suppose that both parties came to the Covenant as equals: indeed it is obvious that in many cases the will of one would prevail over that of the other. A covenant is made between victor and vanquished to restore peaceful relationships, as in 1 Kings 20. 26-34. Ahab has overcome Ben Hadad of Syria, who comes to ask for terms of peace, and offers suggestions.

> And Ahab said, "I will let you go on these terms." So he made a covenant with him, and let him go.

Here it is quite clear that although suggestions are made, their acceptance or rejection is completely at Ahab's discretion, and all through he is the overlord. The making of the covenant restores peaceful relations.

When Jonathan made a covenant with David, it was not a covenant between equals, but between a subject and the heir to the throne. Jonathan makes the covenant and all the initiative and activity comes from him. No recompense is expected from David (1 Sam. 18. 1-4).

In Mal. 2. 14, the covenant relationship is used of

EXODUS FAITH AND COVENANT PEOPLE

marriage. We remember that in Old Testament times the woman was always the inferior partner, and we also remember that marriage is a unity of man and woman as "one flesh" (Gen. 2. 24). There were, of course, covenants between equals, restoring peace where it had been broken, as for instance in Gen. 21. 25ff, and it is worth noticing that there is generally a distinction in terminology. Where a superior makes a covenant with an inferior, it is usually "A made a covenant with B" : where equals are concerned, it is usually "A and B made a covenant". When in 2 Chron. 23. 3 the assembly makes a covenant with the king, it does not break the rule : it simply shows the conception of kingship in Israel, by which the king was invested with authority by the people (cf. 1 Kings 12). In a similar way, we notice that when Josiah publicly declares that he will observe the Law written in the book found in the Temple (2 Kings 23. 1-3), he does not make a Covenant *with* Yahweh, but *before* Yahweh. The Book of the Covenant showed that Yahweh had already made a covenant with Israel (and hence with the king as their leader). All they could do was to accept it, and the covenant made then was between Josiah and the people, in which all joined, to accept God's law.

Enough has been said to show that the idea of a bargain between God and man cannot be sustained. In everything that we say about the covenant, it is important to remember that the initiative is always with God. Even if the relationship is broken time and again from man's side, it still remains valid; if it is to be varied, it is God who must vary it. God's terms stand, and are unchangeable except by God himself.

This idea of a Covenant-making God is not peculiar to Israelite "official" religion. We read, for instance, in Judges 9 of a god worshipped at Shechem called *Baʿal-berith* (Covenant *Baʿal*). Its special emphasis in the Old Testament comes from two factors : first, the character of the God who makes the Covenant; secondly, the way in which covenant thinking permeated every part of Israelite religious thought. It is not too much to say that every aspect of religion has reference to, and is determined by, the covenant faith. To understand the Covenant and its significance is to understand the Old Testament.

What was this Covenant? There are stories of covenants right through the early part of the Bible : with Noah (Gen. 9. 8-17), with Abraham (Gen. 15. 7-21), Isaac (Gen. 17. 19-21) and, according to Ecclus. 17. 1-14, with Adam. These stories come from different strata of Old Testament literature, but the accounts as we have them are all, of course, post-Mosaic. The question arises whether because of the influence of the Mosaic Covenant all earlier history is seen as covenant history, or whether covenant thinking was already well-established in Israel at the time of the Exodus. Taking all the evidence, it seems probable that it is the Mosaic Covenant that is primary, and leads to such radical habits of thought in Israel that when the earlier material comes to be written down, it is coloured through and through with covenant ideas.

The account of the making of the Sinaitic Covenant is found in Exodus, 19—24. These chapters include the so-called "Book of the Covenant" (20. 22—23. 33) an early expansion of the basic Covenant code, which was in all probability a simpler version of the decalogue that we now find in Ex. 20 and Deut. 5. The important points seem to be :

(*a*) The basis of the covenant is God's commandment, which is concerned with both the way in which man should carry out his religious obligations, and the duty which he owes to his fellow men.

(*b*) The terms of the covenant are read to the people, who accept them. There is no suggestion of a "bargain". Nor, in the account of the actual making of the Covenant,

EXODUS FAITH AND COVENANT PEOPLE 11

is there any suggestion of a reciprocal arrangement such as is found in 19. 5, 6 (D).

(*c*) The actual making of the covenant is through the sharing of blood derived from sacrificial beasts. Half the blood is thrown against an altar (i.e. offered to God), and the other half thrown over the people. Though it may seem disgusting to us to-day, the ceremony is analogous to the idea of blood brotherhood : through sharing in the one life (see Lev. 17. 11) the parties are brought together and bound together (see p. 155).

It was the utter conviction of Israel that God was a God who kept his covenant. He had sworn to be their God, and that he would be, no matter how far Israel departed from his will, defied him, or even refused to accept him. On the other hand, they had accepted his covenant, and must take the consequences of breaking it. These consequences were not, as we might expect, the annulment of the Covenant, but the actions of a God who was determined that his purposes should be fulfilled, whatever the cost. The whole history of Israel may be seen in this light : Israel departing from God's covenant, and being brought back through the work of prophets and leaders; Israel learning through suffering the meaning of the call and mission of Yahweh; the way in which they learned more and more of the inwardness of the covenant, and the place in it both of other nations and of men as individuals. The whole of the worship of Israel may be seen as a scheme of maintaining covenant relationship with God, and of restoring it after it had been marred by the sin of man. The hope of the Old Testament is directed towards the time when God will remake his covenant in such a way that it will be kept and not broken (see especially Jer. 31. 31-4), and it is the Christian conviction that this remade covenant came about through the blood of Jesus Christ, shed on the cross, blood which is both offered to God in the sacrifice of perfect obedience, and shared by all who partake through faith in the New Covenant by means of the blood offered to us sacramentally in the Lord's Supper.

The content of a covenant such as this must depend completely on the character of the God who makes the covenant, and to this we now turn.

CHAPTER TWO

THE NATURE OF GOD

> The LORD, the LORD, a God merciful and gracious, slow to anger, and abounding in steadfast love and faithfulness, keeping steadfast love for thousands, forgiving iniquity and transgression and sin, but who will by no means clear the guilty . . . (Ex. 34. 6, 7)

In this chapter we shall look at some of the great concepts of the nature of God found in the Old Testament, noticing in particular how they derive from the Exodus faith, and how in turn they affect the covenant relationship and its demands on the people of God.

THE UNITY OF GOD

> Thus says the LORD, the King of Israel
>   and his redeemer, the LORD of hosts:
> "I am the first and I am the last;
>   besides me there is no god." (Isa. 44. 6)

In this, and similar passages, the Second Isaiah, at the end of the Exile in Babylonia, proclaims the conviction that there is only one God, creator and sustainer of all that exists, and that other so-called gods have no real existence at all. From then on this conviction was never challenged in Israel. Yet, with the possible exception of Egypt for a short period in the fourteenth century B.C. under the "heretic" Pharaoh, Amenhotep IV (Ikhn-aton) (which was much more an acknowledgement of the supreme power of the sun than a true monotheism), Israel was the first nation to reach this conclusion, and they were certainly the first to maintain it as an integral part of their life and theology.

The Second Isaiah was the first in Israel to proclaim this in unmistakable terms, and there can be no doubt that for all practical purposes monotheism was not the faith of pre-Exilic Israel. There is evidence in plenty in the eighth and seventh century prophets to show that the worship of gods other than Yahweh was commonplace, for they have much to say about those who, in taking part in such worship, are breaking the covenant. Nevertheless, monotheistic belief is deeply rooted in Israel's past. The second of the Ten Words (in Jewish reckoning) is "You shall have no other gods before me" (Ex. 20. 3). It is, rightly, pointed out that this does not deny the existence of other gods, it simply insists that to worship them is illegitimate for anyone within the Covenant of Yahweh: to this extent we are here dealing with monolatry rather than monotheism. But as we have seen, Israel's faith is based not only on the Sinaitic Covenant, but also on God's mighty acts in delivering them from Egypt. Here is the crux of the matter. In ancient times, the god of a nation or territory was considered to have power only in his own country and amongst his own people. Outside, he was powerless (cf. 1 Sam. 26. 19; 2 Kings 5. 17). But Yahweh had shown his power and his wonders *in the land of Egypt*, the land where the gods of the Egyptians had sway. Moreover, included in these mighty acts were two in particular which challenged these gods on their own ground—the smiting of the waters of the Nile (Ex. 7. 14-21), and the darkness (Ex. 10. 21-9) overcoming the power of the greatest of them all, Ra, the Sun god.[1] If

---

[1] Even if these stories do not accurately reflect the original events, they come from J and E, the two earliest cycles we have, and clearly show in their presentation the beliefs of the early monarchy.

THE UNITY OF GOD

Yahweh could do this, then he was undoubtedly superior to the gods of Egypt. So, therefore, the prophets condemn completely the political manœuvres of the kings of Israel and Judah in seeking alliances with Egypt: what is their purpose? They have already on their side one who has proved himself far stronger than the Egyptians: to rely on Egypt and not Yahweh is utter disloyalty, since it is a denial of his power, and indeed of the very basis of their national life (cf. e.g. Isa. 30. 1-5). A casual reading of such passages would suggest that Egypt was mistrusted only on political grounds, but it is not so. Condemnation is "religious" just as much as "political".

Not only had Yahweh brought them out of the land of Egypt, he had brought them into Canaan, and had driven out the Canaanites before them. He had shown by the clearest possible proof that he was in control there also. But in spite of this one of the clearest series of events in Hebrew history is that in which the nation took up the worship of the gods of Canaan alongside that of Yahweh, and even began to worship Yahweh as if he were a god of the same sort as them (see pp. 55ff).

The climax of this conflict of Yahwism with the worship of Canaanite gods came in the time of Ahab, with the challenge of Elijah on Mount Carmel to the prophets and worshippers of Ba'al. The point of this story is often stated as being the establishment of the principle of "One God for Israel", and this is true. But it is not the whole story, nor even the most important part. It is often forgotten that Ba'al, too, had his rights in Israel: Jezebel was one of his subjects, and he had a temple and altar in Samaria (on the analogy of 2 Kings 5. 17, there was presumably part of Tyrian soil there as well). Among the prophets of Ba'al many, no doubt, were Tyrians. The test proposed was on Ba'al's own ground, for Ba'al was god of the rain and the storm. Elijah, in the name of Yahweh, withheld rain for three years: the test was whether the storm god could send the lightning to take up a sacrifice prepared for him. On both counts the verdict was clear: Yahweh is greater than Ba'al, and where Yahweh is active, Ba'al has neither rights nor jurisdiction.

The implications are clear. Other gods there may be: they may be all right for other nations. But in comparison with Yahweh they are weak and powerless, and when they come into conflict with him, they might just as well not exist. The matter is taken further by Amos: not only is Yahweh concerned with the sins of other nations (1. 1—2. 3), it is he who is responsible for their migrations, in the same way that he was responsible for Israel's migration from Egypt:

> Did I not bring up Israel from the land of Egypt,
> and the Philistines from Caphtor and the Syrians from Kir?
> (Amos 9. 7)

Isaiah is even more outspoken. Yahweh will use other nations to punish Israel, and will in turn visit their own faults on them:

> Ah, Assyria, the rod of my anger
>   the staff of my fury!
> Against a godless nation I send him,
>   and against the people of my wrath I command him . . .
> When the Lord has finished all his work on Mount Zion and on Jerusalem he will punish the arrogant boasting of the king of Assyria . . . (Isa. 10. 5, 6, 12)

Jeremiah says much the same thing:

> For, lo, I am calling all the tribes of the kingdom of the north, says the LORD; and they shall come and every one shall set his throne at the entrance of the gates of Jerusalem, against all its walls round about, and against all the cities of Judah.
> (Jer. 1. 15)

THE LOVE AND MERCY OF GOD 17

So, when the Second Isaiah says:

> It is he who sits above the circle of the earth,
>   and its inhabitants are like grasshoppers;
> who stretches out the heavens like a curtain,
>   and spreads them like a tent to dwell in;
> who brings princes to nought,
>   and makes the rulers of the earth as nothing. (Isa. 40. 22, 23)

and,

> Thus says the LORD to his anointed, to Cyrus,
>   whose right hand I have grasped,
> to subdue nations before him
>   and ungird the loins of kings . . .
> For the sake of my servant Jacob,
>   and Israel my chosen,
> I call you by your name,
>   I surname you, though you do not know me,
> I am the LORD, and there is no other,
>   besides me there is no God . . .   (Isa. 45. 1, 4, 5)

he is merely stating explicitly what has been for a very long time implicit in Israel's history and faith. It is this belief in the unity of God which makes it possible for Israel to be

> . . . a covenant to the people,
> a light to the nations,
>   to open the eyes that are blind,
> to bring out the prisoners from the dungeon,
>   from the prison those who sit in darkness   (Isa. 42. 6, 7)

and it is on this belief that the whole of later Old Testament and New Testament religion is based.

THE LOVE AND MERCY OF GOD

One of the great words of the Hebrew Old Testament is *chesed*. It is variously translated in the English Versions. "Kindness", "goodness", "mercy" are all used. Coverdale invented the term "loving-kindness" to translate it, and commentators have searched in vain for an adequate translation. No one English word that will do full justice to its meaning, although the translation "devotion" is one which has gained a good deal of favour recently. It is frequently used of relations between man and man, but its most distinctive use is for God's attitude to his people. It is often found, for instance, in the Deuteronomic writings especially, in connection with "covenant":

> Know therefore that the LORD your God is God, the faithful God who keeps covenant and steadfast love (*chesed*) with those who love him and keep his commandments . . .
> (Deut. 7. 9.)

A similar emphasis on the steadfast nature of *chesed* is found in Isa. 40. 6:

> All flesh is grass,
>   and all its beauty is like the flower of the field . .
> The grass withers, the flower fades;
>   but the word of our God will stand for ever.

Where the Revised Standard Version has "beauty", and the English Authorized and Revised versions have "goodliness" the Hebrew has *chesed*. The prophet is comparing the qualities of men with those of God. The steadfastness of men is no more than the life of the wild flowers: it is compared with the word of Yahweh which will stand for ever.

We must note this close connection between *chesed* and the covenant, the expression of God's eternal purpose for Israel. We may almost say that the *chesed* of God is the application of his total nature in dealing with his people. The various nuances of meaning of *chesed* will help us understand this nature of God.

It is applied to God's gift of good things to his people, especially the good life:

> Hearken diligently to me, and eat what is good,
>   and delight yourselves in fatness.

Incline your ear, and come to me;
   hear, that your soul may live;
And I will make with you an everlasting covenant,
   my steadfast, sure love for David (*chesedim*, "mercies").
                                 (Isa. 55. 2, 3)

to God's help in trouble and distress :

> For we are bondmen; yet our God has not forsaken us in our bondage, but has extended to us his steadfast love (*chesed*) before the kings of Persia, to grant us some reviving to set up the house of our God, to repair its ruins, and to give us protection in Judea and Jerusalem.   (Ezra 9. 9)

in preserving life from death :

> Turn, O LORD, save my life;
>   deliver me for the sake of thy steadfast love (*chesed*).
> For in death there is no remembrance of thee . . . (Ps. 6. 4, 5)

in saving men from sin :

> Have mercy on me, O God,
>   according to they steadfast love (*chesed*);
> according to thy abundant mercy
>   blot out my transgressions.   (Ps. 51. 1)

in teaching men the ways of God :

> Deal with thy servant according to thy steadfast love (*chesed*),
>   and teach me thy statutes.   (Ps. 119. 124)

We can get some idea of the ordinary meaning of the word by seeing how it is used of the relationship between man and man. Even if man is not like God, we can be certain that the *chesed* of God will be not less than that of men. With men, it is first and foremost that of *loyalty* :

> Many a man proclaims his own loyalty (*chesed*),
>   but a faithful man who can find?   (Prov. 20. 6)

If I am still alive, show me the loyal love (*chesed*) of the LORD, that I may not die; and do not cut off your loyalty (*chesed*) from my house for ever. When the LORD cuts off every one of the enemies of David from the face of the earth, let not the name of Jonathan be cut off from the house of David. (1 Sam. 20. 14-16)

We remember particularly the covenant relationship between Jonathan and David.

It is concerned with *kindness*:

> A man who is kind (*lit.* "a man of *chesed*") benefits himself,
> but a cruel man hurts himself. (Prov. 11. 17)

> For he did not remember to show kindness (*chesed*),
> but pursued the poor and needy
> and the brokenhearted to their death. (Ps. 109. 16)

where clearly there is an element of "mercy" in our modern sense also.

We also find the meaning of *piety*, that is, living a life in conformity with the ways of Yahweh:

> For I desire steadfast love (*chesed*) and not sacrifice,
> the knowledge of God, rather than burnt offerings.
> (Hos. 6. 6)

This meaning is found particularly in the related adjective *chasid*, which in the great majority of cases means "pious" rather than "merciful" or "kind":

> Therefore let every one who is godly (*chasid*) offer prayer to
> thee (Ps. 32. 6)

> Sing praises to the LORD, O you his saints (*chasidim*),
> and give thanks to his holy name. (Ps. 30. 4)

Eventually this word *chasidim*, with its literal meaning "pious ones", came to be applied as a technical term to the party which opposed the spread of Greek influence in the second century B.C., and joined the Maccabees in their fight against Antiochus Epiphanes (see, e.g. 1 Macc. 2. 42

THE LOVE AND MERCY OF GOD

and margin), a party which became the ancestors of the Pharisees of New Testament times.

We may sum up by saying that *chesed* is that quality of faithfulness which expresses itself in seeking the good of one's fellows. It is also used of the relationship between man and God. On man's side, it implies remaining faithful to God, to his ordinances and statutes. On God's side, it is his quality in remaining always the same unchangeable God, and maintaining his purposes for Israel and mankind in general, even though they neglect his ways. It is difficult to resist the conclusion that the *chesed* God shows to man demands the response of showing *chesed* to other men. The books of the Law, especially the Book of the Covenant (Ex. 20. 22—23. 22) and the Book of Deuteronomy, are full of the duties which men owe to each other, and to obey this law is to be *chasid*, pious. In other words, because God is what he is, men are required to live together within his covenant community in a way which reflects the nature of the Covenant God.

However, *chesed* is in some ways an impersonal quality: it has not that intense emotional content that is usually associated with "love". There are a number of Hebrew words signifying "love" in this more personal sense, of which the most important is the verb *'aheb*. This word, commonly used of the relations between individuals, does not seem to have been used of God's attitude to men before Hosea. It is Hosea who sees the covenant relationship between Yahweh and the nation under the intensely personal figure of marriage (cf. e.g. Hos. 1—3), and it is not, therefore, surprising that he should also use the verb of human love to describe God's love to his people:

> And the LORD said to me, "Go again, love a woman who is beloved of a paramour and is an adulteress; even as the LORD loves the people of Israel, though they turn to other gods . . .
> (Hos. 3. 1)

where in each case the verb is *'aheb*. Or again:

> When Israel was a child, I loved him,
>   and out of Egypt I called my son. (Hos. 11. 1)
>
> Because of the wickedness of their deeds
>   I will drive them out of my house.
> I will love them no more;
>   all their princes are rebels. (Hos. 9. 15)

It is, however, closely connected with *chesed*:

> Thus says the LORD: ...
> I have loved (*'aheb*) you with an everlasting love (*'ahabah*);
>   therefore I have continued my faithfulness (*chesed*) to you.
> (Jer. 31. 2, 3)

This love is not because Israel is a particularly lovable nation; nor is it a sentimental love which does not care what the beloved is like. It is a love which comes completely from God's own free choice, and which demands that those loved shall *become* lovely in keeping the ways of Yahweh:

> For you are a people holy to the LORD your God; the LORD your God has chosen you to be a people for his own possession, out of all the peoples that are on the face of the earth. It was not because you were more in number than any other people that the LORD set his love [2] upon you and chose you, for you were the fewest of all peoples; but it is because the LORD loves (*'aheb*) you, and is keeping the oath which he swore to your fathers ... Know therefore that the LORD your God is God, the faithful God who keeps covenant and steadfast love (*chesed*) with those who love (*'aheb*) him and keep his commandments ... (Deut. 7. 6-9)

It may be added here that love will imply correction, even if it is painful:

> My son, do not despise the LORD's discipline
>   or be weary of his reproof,
> for the LORD reproves him whom he loves (*'aheb*) ...
> (Prov. 3. 11, 12)

[2] *Chashaq*, a word very similar in meaning to *'aheb*.

This applies to Israel also:

> You only have I known
>   of all the families of the earth;
> therefore I will punish you
>   for all your iniquities.   (Amos 3. 2)

But this punishment was never impersonal: it was always mixed with loving care and tenderness, seeking only the good of the beloved:

> In all their affliction he was afflicted,
>   and the angel of his presence saved them;
> in his love (*'ahabah*) and in his pity he redeemed them . . .
>   (Isa. 63. 9)

It is here that we come to our next point, the justice of God. To be lovely, his people must show other characteristics of Yahweh, notably *righteousness*. The purpose of his love (and chastisement) is therefore, to make them a righteous people, else it will have failed.

THE JUSTICE OF GOD

Except in a very few cases, the words "just" and "justice" stand for the Hebrew words which are also translated "righteous" and "righteousness" (*tsedeq* and *tsedaqah*). The basic meaning is "that which is as it should be". It is used of weights and measures:

> You shall have just balances, a just ephah, and a just bath.
>   (Ezek. 45. 10)

no short measure here! In the Law Court:

> You shall do no injustice in judgement; you shall not be partial to the poor or defer to the great, but in righteousness shall you judge your neighbour.   (Lev. 19. 15)

that is, judgement is to be given according to the right

standard of conformity to truth rather than by the wrong standard of favouritism.

A good example, often misinterpreted, comes from the 23rd Psalm:

> He makes me lie down in green pastures.
> He leads me beside still waters . . .
> He leads me in paths of righteousness . . .

The whole context makes it quite clear that the Psalmist is not referring to religious ideas: he is trusting in Yahweh to bring him to the very best pastures and the waters where he can be sure of finding drink for his flocks; and to lead him in the best way, on paths that are as they should be, which lead to the shepherd's destination and do not send him astray, which are not overgrown with thorns and thistles and do not go through impassable places.

It is this idea of *normality* which leads us straight to the main meaning. For Israel, the normal is that which is in accordance with the will of Yahweh. As with *chesed*, God's righteousness means that he always acts in accordance with his character, and expects his people to do the same. If we are to understand the righteousness of God, we must see what he demands from his people. A good starting point will be the book of Amos, often known as "the prophet of righteousness". Israel is condemned, for they

> . . . turn justice to wormwood.
> and cast down righteousness (*tsedaqah*) to the earth!
>
> (Amos 5. 7)

instead of doing what is required:

> But let justice roll down like waters,
>   and righteousness like an everflowing stream. (Amos 5. 24)

A brief look through the book will show what lack of justice involved. Bad administration of the law (5. 12), oppression of the poor (2. 6. 7), sexual irregularities (2. 7), neglect of the word of Yahweh (2. 12), social injustice

THE JUSTICE OF GOD

involving luxury in the midst of poverty (4. 1; 6. 4-6), formalism in religion (4. 4, 5; 5. 21-4), idolatry (5. 25, 26), cheating in the market (8. 4-6), and so on. It is a bitter indictment. But the point is that the people of Yahweh ought to have known better : they had had the experience of the Exodus; they had been warned by prophets and men of God. The punishment would therefore be the more severe (2. 6, 9-16; 3. 1, 2).

Although this requirement of just dealing is emphasized strongly in Amos, it would be a great mistake to think of his teaching as an innovation. It goes right back to the desert tradition, to the Exodus itself. They had been forced into slavery, and rescued : would they enslave others (Ex. 21. 16)? They had been wronged : would they wrong others (Ex.. 22. 21ff; 23. 9)? Six of the Ten Words are concerned with social relationships. Right through their history in Palestine, the emphasis on right dealing socially and religiously stands out.

Eli and his house were cut off because of the sins of his sons (1 Sam. 2. 22-5; 3. 10-14). David, the perfect king of Israel, a man after God's own heart, is condemned by Nathan in the name of Yahweh for the episode of Bathsheba and Uriah (2 Sam. 11. 2—12. 25). This story is important. It is not only that the prophet of God rebukes sin, but that David accepts the rebuke and repents. In any other nation at the time, it would have been the accepted thing for the king to take any woman he wished : if her husband were in the way . . . ! Had a prophet dared to remonstrate, it would in all probability have been the last thing he did. But this was not the Israelite tradition, and David accepts the rebuke of Yahweh.

This comparison between the ways of Israel and those of other nations is very clear in the story of Elijah, Ahab, Jezebel, and Naboth's vineyard (1 Kings 21). The "normal" attitude is that of Jezebel, who cannot understand Ahab's qualms in the matter. *She* has no hesitation in doing away with a prophet of Yahweh (1 Kings 19. 2), nor in committing murder to get her own way. Ahab, however, knew all along that the whole sordid affair was wrong, and is reluctant to have anything to do with it—at least until after the deed was done. He, too, accepts the rebuke of the prophet and repents. Here is a concept of righteousness which depends not on social custom but on the nature of Yahweh. In no other country at this time could there have been any conflict between the will of the king and the will of the god, since an almost universal feature of life in the Fertile Crescent at this time was a close identification of god with king, either as incarnation or vicegerent.

Amos, then, spoke to a people who ought not to have been ignorant of the moral demands of Yahweh. His words are echoed by all the other pre-Exilic prophets. It is worth noticing what the result of unrighteousness will be:

> The high places of Isaac shall be made desolate,
>   and the sanctuaries of Israel shall be laid waste,
>   and I will rise against the house of Jeroboam with the sword.
> (Amos. 7. 9)

> "Therefore I will take you into exile beyond Damascus," says
>   the LORD.   (Amos. 5. 27)

> They shall return to the land of Egypt,
>   and Assyria shall be their king,
>   because they have refused to return to me.
> The sword shall rage against their cities,
>   consume the bars of their gates,
>   and devour them in their fortresses.   (Hos. 11. 5, 6)

Nevertheless, God will not give up his people completely:

> How can I give you up, O Ephraim!
>   How can I hand you over, O Israel! ...
> I will not execute my fierce anger,
>   I will not again destroy Ephraim;
>   ... I will not come to destroy.   (Hos. 11. 8, 9)

THE JUSTICE OF GOD 27

The contradiction here is apparent rather than real. God stands in a covenant relationship with Israel which he cannot break, because to do so would be false to himself. His righteousness demands that unrighteousness be punished: his love demands that the unlovely be chastened until they become lovely. In other words, God's purposes for Israel remain, but because of the degeneration of the people, they will be fulfilled in a different way. The story of the events leading to the Exile emphasizes that God is using these happenings quite deliberately to take the people out of the surroundings in which apostasy is inevitable, in order to learn in a different atmosphere just who God was and what he demanded. They could then return for a new start. The punishment and exile of the people are not a denial of the righteousness and *chesed* of God, but their expression and fulfilment.

Let us now take up another point. In the circumstances of Israel under the monarchy, unrighteousness always bore hardest on the poor and needy. The rich and powerful could—and did—stand up for themselves. "Injustice" and "oppression" are in many places synonymous terms. God's righteousness, then, is shown by his always being on the side of the poor and helpless:

> Arise, O LORD; O God lift up thy hand;
>   forget not the afflicted.
> . . . The hapless commits himself to thee;
>   thou hast been the helper of the fatherless. (Ps. 10. 12, 14)

> "Because the poor are despoiled, because the needy groan,
>   I will now arise," says the LORD;
> "I will place him in the safety for which he longs." (Ps. 12. 5)

This is true not only in his dealings with individuals, but with Israel. When Israel is groaning under oppression, and when they have learned their lesson through the chastening of adversity, then his righteousness will express itself once more in salvation :

> Who gave up Jacob to the spoiler,
>   and Israel to the robbers?
> Was it not the LORD, against whom we have sinned,
>   in whose ways they would not walk,
>   and whose law they would not obey?
> So he poured upon him the heat of his anger
>   and the might of battle . . .
> But now thus says the LORD,
>   he who created you, O Jacob,
>   he who formed you, O Israel.
> "Fear not, for I have redeemed you . . ."   (Isa. 42. 24—43. 1)

In the later stages of Old Testament history, righteousness comes to have a slightly different meaning. We have seen how those with *chesed*, the *chasidim*, developed into the sect of the Pharisees. As part of this movement, righteousness came to be equated with the keeping of *Torah*. This word is often misused and mistranslated as if it meant "law", and the Pentateuch, known to the Jews as *Torah*, thought of as a code of rules. To the Jew, however, *Torah* is much more "a way of life", "instruction", "the will of God". It is not a code of rules to be kept but a way of life to be followed. Perhaps the best commentary on what *Torah* meant, and means, to the pious Jew is Ps. 119. This outlook contrasts strongly with the legalistic view usually associated with the Pharisee. That legalism was common among Pharisees, we need not doubt : it is always present in any ethical religion. But it would be quite wrong to condemn all Pharisees, much less all Judaism, on the grounds of legalism. The Jewish ideal is that the will of God shall be carried into every aspect of life, and that his conduct in every detail shall be brought under *Torah*, and it is an ideal that might well be learned by many who profess and call themselves Christians.

THE HOLINESS OF GOD

And one called to another and said:
  "Holy, holy, holy is the LORD of hosts;
  the whole earth is full of his glory."
And I said: "Woe is me! For I am lost; for I am a man of unclean lips, and I dwell in the midst of a people of unclean lips; for my eyes have seen the King, the LORD of hosts!"
(Isa. 6. 3, 5)

The concept of the holiness of God shown in this passage, that he was a being so utterly different from men that he could not be touched, approached, or even seen without grave danger, is one which goes back to the very earliest strata of religion (though, as we shall see, it is enormously deepened by Isaiah). The word for "holiness", *qodesh*, has as its root meaning "separateness". Yahweh is holy because he is God and not man, and people, places, and things are holy because they are set apart for him, or because he is thought to be there. It is important to realize that during a large part of the history of Israel, holiness has no moral connotation whatever. When we read:

There shall be no cult prostitute of the daughters of Israel, neither shall there be a cult prostitute of the sons of Israel.
(Deut. 23. 17)

we say, "Very right and proper!" When they are turned out of the Temple by Josiah, we fail to see why it had not happened earlier:

And he broke down the houses of the cult prostitutes (masc.) which were in the house of the LORD . . . (2 Kings 23. 7)

It comes as a shock to realize that the strict translation of "cult prostitute" is "holy man" or "holy woman"!

It is Isaiah who really takes hold of the idea of holiness and links it with the love and righteousness of God. Look again at the passage with which we started. Isaiah is confronted with the vision of the holiness of Yahweh, and he cries out in terror: but it is *not* because he has seen Yahweh, but because he is unclean *morally*. Uncleanness, of course, was well understood: before there could be contact with any holy place or thing certain ritual demands had to be met (cf. e.g., 1 Sam. 21. 4-6), and to touch a holy thing without due preparation might well be dangerous (cf. 2 Sam. 6. 6-8). But now it was not ritual defilement, but unclean *lips*.

For Isaiah, Yahweh was indeed different from men, and was holy. But the difference was shown especially in that Yahweh was righteous and men were not:

> But the LORD of hosts is exalted in justice,
>   and the Holy God shows himself holy in righteousness.
>
> (Isa. 5. 16)

Isaiah's characteristic term for Yahweh is "the Holy One of Israel", and he demands holiness from his people. That is, before man can approach God he must purify himself not only ritually but morally:

> When you come to appear before me,
>   who requires of you
>   this trampling of my courts?
> Bring no more vain offerings . . .
> When you spread forth your hands,
>   I will hide my eyes from you;
> even though you make many prayers,
>   I will not listen;
>   your hands are full of blood.
> Wash yourselves; make yourselves clean;
>   remove the evil of your doings
>   from before my eyes;
> cease to do evil,
>   learn to do good;
> seek justice,

THE HOLINESS OF GOD

>   correct oppression;
> defend the fatherless,
>   plead for the widow. (Isa. 1. 12, 13, 15-17)

This idea of moral as well as ritual holiness finds expression in the so-called "Holiness Code" (Lev. ch. 17—26), which probably reached its present form in the seventh century B.C. and was afterwards incorporated into the Priestly Code. It is in this code, in which a good deal of material is concerned with matters of ritual purity and impurity and of ceremonial cleansing (e.g. 22. 5-9), that we find the commandment:

> You shall be holy; for I the LORD your God am holy.
> (Lev. 19. 2)

which is not to be interpreted merely in terms of ritual holiness, as the rest of the chapter shows:

> You shall not steal, nor deal falsely, nor lie to one another (v. 11).
> You shall do no injustice in judgement; you shall not be partial to the poor or defer to the great, but in righteousness shall you judge your neighbour (v. 15).

Examples could be multiplied.

From this time on, ritual is closely connected with morality, as for instance in the regulations for the Day of Atonement, the day of ceremonial cleansing of the nation, we find:

> ... Aaron shall lay both his hands upon the head of the live goat, and confess over him all the iniquities of the people of Israel, and all their transgressions, all their sins ...
> (Lev. 16. 21)

In this, the Jews made one of the great advances of history. It is only necessary to read some of the things done in the name of religion in the fertility cults of the Fertile Crescent to realize the difference between that sort of religion and the faith of Israel. Nor is the connection of religion with morality stronger in the religions of Greece and Rome, or in Oriental religions. It is true that in Greece and Rome, India and China, thinking men came to see that religion without morality is useless. But their solution on the whole was to substitute for religion a philosophical or mystical system that almost ceases to be a religion at all. It is the merit of Isaiah of Jerusalem and those who followed him that they were able to combine the two. But it is not their doing only. It stems from the faith handed down to them, so that in reality Isaiah is simply carrying to their logical conclusion ideas and teachings which are rooted right back in the Exodus tradition.

GOD THE SAVIOUR AND REDEEMER

> ... there is no other god besides me,
>   a righteous God and a Saviour;
>   there is none besides me.
> Turn to me and be saved,
>   all the ends of the earth!
>   For I am God, and there is no other.   (Isa. 45. 21, 22)

If Israel did not know Yahweh as Saviour they had no excuse, for the whole of their history emphasizes this aspect of his work. He had saved them from Egypt, he had brought them into Canaan, in countless events he had shown that he was with them to save them, even though they rejected him:

> Thus says the LORD, the God of Israel, "I brought up Israel out of Egypt, and I delivered you from the hand of the Egyptians and from the hand of all the kingdoms that were oppressing you." But you have this day rejected your God, who saves you from all your calamities and your distresses ...
> (1 Sam. 10. 18, 19)

During the early part of their history in Palestine, Israel thought of Yahweh as a God who would save them from

GOD THE SAVIOUR AND REDEEMER

their enemies whatever they did. They looked for the Day of Yahweh, when all would be well with them. It takes Amos to insist that, since God is righteous, the day of his visitation is likely to be for judgement rather than for salvation (cf. Amos 5. 18-20, etc.). For Amos, this is enough; but for Hosea it is not enough. God is a God of *chesed* as well as of righteousness, and he cannot cast off his people as easily as that. The analogy of his marriage which we find in chs. 1—3 of his book shows us how deeply he feels both the sin of the people and the love of God. Israel is a harlot of a nation which has forsaken Yahweh and followed the gods of Canaan (2. 5). Yahweh cannot tolerate this: he will take them away from their land after punishment (2. 9-13), where there will be a reforming of the nation, when they will once more realize their Exodus faith and respond to God:

> Therefore, behold, I will allure her,
> and bring her into the wilderness,
> and speak tenderly to her . . .
> And there she shall answer as in the days of her youth,
> as at the time when she came out of the land of Egypt.
> (Hos. 2. 14, 15)

as a result of which,

> . . . . I will betroth you to me for ever; I will betroth you to me in righteousness and in justice, in steadfast love, and in mercy . . . and you shall know the LORD. (Hos. 2. 19, 20)

It is clear, however, that neither complete destruction nor salvation for the entire nation will meet the case, and Isaiah takes the next step in the idea of the *remnant*. The remnant will be those who remain after the calamity coming to overtake the nation:

> In that day the Lord will extend his hand yet a second time to recover the remnant which is left of his people, from Assyria, from Egypt . . . and from the coastlands of the sea.

And there will be a highway from Assyria
   for the remnant which is left of his people,
as there was for Israel
   when they came up from the land of Egypt.   (Isa. 11. 11, 16)

There is no suggestion that the remnant will be saved because they are, at the time of the catastrophe, particularly righteous or faithful. Rather, because they are the remnant, they will understand the power of Yahweh and return to him:

> In that day the remnant of Israel and the survivors of the house of Jacob will no more lean upon him that smote them, but will lean upon the LORD, the Holy One of Israel, in truth. A remnant will return, the remnant of Jacob, to the mighty God. For though your people Israel be as the sand of the sea, only a remnant of them will return. Destruction is decreed, overflowing with righteousness.   (Isa. 10. 20-2)[3]

After destruction, the righteousness of God will manifest itself in the righteousness of the remnant:

> In that day the branch of the LORD shall be beautiful and glorious, and the fruit of the land shall be the pride and glory of the survivors of Israel. And he who is left in Zion and remains in Jerusalem will be called holy, everyone who has been recorded for life in Jerusalem, when the Lord shall have washed away the filth of the daughters of Zion and cleansed the bloodstains of Jerusalem from its midst by a spirit of judgment and by a spirit of burning.   (Isa. 4. 2-4)

It is a matter of history that the main stream of Hebrew religion was carried on in the Southern Kingdom, Judah, after the fall of Samaria; that in 597 and 586 Jerusalem was captured by the Babylonians; and that the leaders of Judah were carried into exile in Babylonia. It was to this "remnant" and their descendants that Isaiah's greater

[3] Although the actual Isaianic authorship of this passage is disputed, the "remnant" teaching is fully in harmony with his thought.

GOD THE SAVIOUR AND REDEEMER

successor was to speak. Before we turn to the exile, however, we must notice another aspect of Isaiah's teaching which was to assume great importance later—the beginning of what is often called the "messianic hope".

We all know the way in which passages from Isaiah are read at Christmas as "prophecies of the messiah". But if we look more carefully at these passages we may come to suspect, to put it no more strongly, that Christian tradition has read more into them than they can really bear in their context. The famous passage in 7. 14 has, of course, no reference to Christ at all, as is clear if the whole chapter is read. What of the others?

Isaiah looks forward to the return of the remnant in righteousness, when the will of Yahweh will be universally obeyed in Israel, and when his holiness and righteousness will be fully manifest. This ideal period will be symbolized by an ideal governor, who will show in his acts the character of Yahweh. In 9. 2-7 he draws a picture of this ideal king in words familiar to all: a similar picture is drawn in 32. 1-8. Some have identified this picture with the infant Hezekiah. However this may be, there is nothing in either passage to suggest that the ideal age is to be *inaugurate*d by this person; rather, he is a symptom of it. To be consistent with Isaiah's thought, we have to say that the new age is to be inaugurated by Yahweh himself.

We ought, too, to refer to the passage in 11. 1-9. This is closely connected with the rest of the chapter, and it may well be much later than Isaiah of Jerusalem. But however this may be, we ought to note the thought that it is not only among men that the will of God will be done—it will extend to the natural order also: righteousness and peace will cover the whole of creation. The earlier verses in the chapter at first sight refer to an individual who will bring about this state of affairs, although the term "messiah" is not used. Further thought, however may suggest that it is not impossible that the "shoot from the stump of Jesse" refers not to an individual but to the righteous remnant who will spring out of the wreck of destruction and will inaugurate the new age.

We may sum up by saying, then, that though we find in Isaiah the beginning of an expectation that the ideal time will be closely connected with an ideal ruler, we are not justified in finding any reference to an individual who will inaugurate this golden age. This development will only come much later.

When the "best of the people" were taken into exile, the hopes of the nation went with them. Although only a small minority, they included almost all who were able to lead in thought or action. To them the message of Ezekiel came. The warnings of doom had come horribly true—the task of the prophets was now to make them realize that God would also fulfil his promises of salvation:

> Thus says the LORD: I will gather you from the peoples, and assemble you out of the countries where you have been scattered . . . And I will give them one heart, and put a new spirit within them: I will take the stony heart out of their flesh and give them a heart of flesh, that they may walk in my statutes and keep my ordinances and obey them; and they shall be my people, and I will be their God. (Ezek. 11. 17, 19)

National salvation in terms of return to Jerusalem is linked by Ezekiel with a return to the ways of Yahweh. In this, he is simply applying the principles of the remnant, and echoing what Jeremiah had said before him:

> Behold the days are coming, says the LORD, when I will make a new covenant with the house of Israel and with the house of Judah, not like the covenant which I made with their fathers when I took them by the hand to bring them out of the land of Egypt, my covenant which they broke, though I was their husband, says the LORD. But this is the covenant which I will make with the house of Israel after those days,

says the LORD: I will put my law within them, and I will write it upon their hearts; and I will be their God, and they shall be my people ... for they shall all know me, from the least of them to the greatest, says the LORD; for I will forgive their iniquity, and I will remember their sin no more. (Jer. 31. 31-4)

The emphasis on the spiritual return of the people is seen especially in the vision of the valley of dry bones (Ezek. 37. 1-14). It is emphasized, too, that salvation will come from God alone:

For thus says the Lord GOD: Behold, I, myself will search for my sheep, and will seek them out. As a shepherd seeks out his flock when some of his sheep have been scattered abroad, so will I seek out my sheep; and I will rescue them from all places where they have been scattered ... I will bring them out from the peoples, and gather them from the countries, and will bring them into their own land; and I will feed them on the mountains of Israel ... I myself will be the shepherd of my sheep, and I will make them lie down, says the Lord GOD. I will seek the lost, and I will bring back the strayed, and I will bind up the crippled, and I will strengthen the weak, and the fat and the strong I will watch over; I will feed them in justice. (Ezek. 34. 11-16)

It is in the Second Isaiah, however, that we expect and find most about the salvation of Yahweh. The prophet was announcing, not that salvation *would* come, but that it *had* come, and was now present, and that his hearers were to receive it. His task is to convince them that, in spite of all appearances to the contrary, God is working for them:

... there is no other god besides me,
  a righteous God and a saviour;
  there is none besides me.
Turn to me and be saved,
  all the ends of the earth!
  For I am God, and there is no other.
By myself I have sworn,
  from my mouth has gone forth in righteousness

a word that shall not return:
"To me every knee shall bow,
every tongue shall swear." (Isa. 45. 21-3)

We have looked at this passage before in considering the unity of God. In it come together the ideas we have already noticed of God's steadfastness, righteousness, and holiness, and they do so in terms of salvation. Because God is what he is, he will save. He is not a saviour *in spite of* being righteous, but *because* he is righteous. Those addressed are the remnant:

Hearken to me, O house of Jacob,
all the remnant of the house of Israel,
who have been borne by me from your birth,
carried from the womb;
even to your old age I am He,
and to grey hairs I will carry you.
I have made, and I will bear;
I will carry and will save. (Isa. 46. 3, 4)

The sin which caused the exile is now purged:

Comfort, comfort my people,
says your God.
Speak tenderly to Jerusalem,
and cry to her
that her warfare is ended,
and her iniquity is pardoned. (Isa. 40. 1, 2)

and the promised salvation is actually *here*:

Behold the Lord GOD comes with might,
and his arm rules for him;
behold, his reward is with him,
and his recompense before him.
He will feed his flock like a shepherd . . . (Isa. 40. 10, 11)

We also find introduced a new conception:

I will help you, says the LORD;
your Redeemer is the Holy One of Israel. (Isa. 41. 14)

GOD THE SAVIOUR AND REDEEMER

We need to look closely at the word "redeemer", for it is used a great deal in Christian theology, and a misunderstanding of its Biblical use, both in the Old Testament and the New, can lead to trouble. The word in Hebrew is *go'el*, which is the active participle of the verb *ga'al*. The obvious meaning is "one who buys back", and it certainly has this meaning in many places:

> If your brother becomes poor, and sells part of his property, then his next of kin shall come and redeem what his brother has sold. (Lev. 25. 25)

> All that opens the womb is mine, all your male cattle, the firstlings of cow and sheep. The firstlings of an ass you shall redeem with a lamb, or if you will not redeem it you shall break its neck. All the first-born of your sons you shall redeem . . . (Ex. 34. 19, 20)

It is important to notice that the word translated "next of kin" in Leviticus is *go'el*. The point is that the next of kin has a duty to buy back any family property that has been alienated. A good example is found in Ruth 3. 1—4. 6, where Boaz offers the right of redemption to Ruth's next of kin. When he refuses, Boaz, as next in line, takes the duty on himself.

The duties of next of kin are not, however, confined to the redemption of property. He is bound to raise up a family for the dead man if he had no heir. This typical Hebrew institution of Levirate marriage is referred to in Matt. 22. 23ff, and is described in Deut. 25. 5-10. It is the *go'el* who takes blood revenge when necessary (Deut. 19. 6, 12; Num. 35. 19ff). The primary meaning of *ga'al* therefore seems to be not "redeem" but "act as near kinsman", with the primary task of putting things right. The emphasis is not on buying back, but on restoring things as they ought to be; any idea of payment is incidental.

When we refer to God as redeemer, this is the emphasis. He is restoring things to what they ought to be in his divine plan: he is putting things right. A similar usage is found in the well-known passage in Job 19. 25:

> For I know that my redeemer lives.

Job is not referring to a future life: he is saying that even though he dies, he is convinced that God will vindicate his memory, and that the record will be put straight.

The Second Isaiah, therefore, sees God as the one who will restore Israel to her place in his plan. The price paid is indeed mentioned in one passage:

> For I am the LORD your God,
>   the Holy One of Israel, your Saviour.
> I give Egypt as your ransom,
>   Ethiopia and Seba in exchange for you. (Isa. 43. 3)

Taken in the context of the whole book, the implication is that in order to make certain that Israel returns to Palestine, Cyrus is being called to take over control of a large empire. The passage is not emphasizing the ransom price, but that in spite of all appearances what really matters in the career of Cyrus is not world conquest, as appears on the surface, but the restoration of Israel. It is an expression of the faith of the prophet in Yahweh's control of history.[4]

Taken with his uncompromising emphasis on monotheism, Deutero-Isaiah's teaching on God as Saviour leads him to insist that salvation is for all peoples (45. 21-5), emphasized by the teaching that

> I will give you as a light to the nations,
>   that my salvation may reach to the end of the earth.
> (Isa. 49. 6)

[4] It has been argued (by Professor A. R. Johnson) that *ga'al* has a root meaning of "cover", and that in these passages the right translation of *go'el* is "protector". In so far as the function of a protector is to maintain the right, the effect is not very different, but there can be no doubt that in many places "protector" gives very good sense.

GOD THE SAVIOUR AND REDEEMER   41

This verse comes from the second of the four "Servant Songs", passages which from the Christian viewpoint are probably the most important in the Old Testament. They have probably been subjected to more intense study and attempts at interpretation than any other part of the Old Testament. This is not the place for a full discussion;[5] the interpretation given here is the one which seems most likely to the present writer. The passages in question are 42. 1-4 (& 5-9); 49. 1-6; 50. 4-9; and 52. 13—53. 12. We may note that in the Second Song (49. 4) the Servant is identified as Israel. This has been challenged by some as a later interpolation; but even so the Servant=Israel equation is found in other parts of the book (e.g., 41. 8; 44. 1). Many have suggested that all through the songs the Servant is the personified nation (this is the traditional Jewish interpretation). Now let us turn to the songs.

In the first, Israel, the servant, is called in order to bring justice to the whole earth. This is to be done not by military might, but by tenderness and faithfulness. In the second song this mission to the world is combined with a mission to Israel. They have not yet understood the meaning of servanthood: moreover, the servant's mission is meeting with little success. Clearly, the mission of Israel as servant is to be fulfilled by only a minority of the nation. This minority is not the remnant, for as we have seen, the whole group of returned exiles will constitute the remnant; nevertheless remnant thinking has certainly influenced the prophet's thought. Now, so far there has been no suggestion that the servant is a *suffering* servant, even though his mission has been rejected. In the third song, however, rejection has become actual persecution, and in the fourth song, death. It is extremely difficult to think of the fourth song except as having reference to a single individual.

[5] For which see North, C. R., *The Suffering Servant in Deutero-Isaiah*, 2nd ed., Oxford 1956.

Reconstructing the thought of the prophet, we may say that he thinks of Israel as having a servant mission to the world. This is realized and accepted only by a minority, who find that in obeying God they have the task of converting the major part of their own nation as well as taking the message of Yahweh to the world. This attempt at conversion is rejected, and actual persecution results, which in all probability leads to a further falling away. In the fourth song it is difficult to be sure whether the servant is an actual man who has suffered death for the nation, or whether, as seems more probable, the experience of persecution which the prophet himself has had leads him to believe that when a man comes who completely accepts and obeys the will of God, the only result will be utter rejection and death. Yet through that, God's purposes will be achieved, not only in Israel, but throughout the world (52. 15). Yet it is important to realize that the servant is doing this as part of Israel on behalf of Israel; indeed, if we think of Israel as the people who remain faithful to the covenant, he *is* the ideal Israel. Whether this suggests a messianic interpretation of the servant songs depends on what we mean by "messiah". It is clear that the prophet is not consciously looking forward to the work of Jesus, yet equally clear that the life of Jesus is a fulfilment of this prophecy. What is important, however, is to notice the place which is ascribed to Israel in God's plan of salvation.

It was, however, a mission which post-Exilic Israel failed to realize. There were many reasons why Israel should turn in on itself, and the Jews should try to maintain their nationality by insisting on their exclusive nature as the (privileged) chosen people of God. Even where the idea of the world-mission of Israel is maintained, it is not in terms of servanthood, but of a supreme nation receiving the homage of the rest of the world, seeking in Israel safety from the wrath of Yahweh :

GOD THE SAVIOUR AND REDEEMER

> . . . nations shall come to your light,
> and kings to the brightness of your rising.   (Isa. 60. 3)

> Aliens shall stand and feed your flocks,
> foreigners shall be your ploughmen and vinedressers;
> but you shall be called the priests of the LORD . . . (Isa. 61. 5, 6)

see also 60. 10-16. Or again,

> Many peoples and strong nations shall come to seek the LORD of hosts in Jerusalem, and to entreat the favour of the LORD. Thus says the LORD of hosts: In those days ten men from the nations of every tongue shall take hold of the robe of a Jew, saying, "Let us go with you, for we have heard that God is with you."   (Zech. 8. 22, 23)

There were, of course, protests against this way of thinking. One is found in Isa. 61. 1-4, a passage with clear affinities with the Servant Songs, although the following verses revert to the later idea. Again, the book of Jonah is a standing protest against all narrow exclusiveness. But on the whole the exclusive interpretation prevailed.

It was during the post-exilic period that a further development of messianic thought appeared. The nation had returned to Palestine, but the good time hoped for did not materialize. They were (except for a brief period under the Maccabees) a subject nation, and prosperity and peace seemed as far away as ever. It is not surprising that they started to look forward once more to Yahweh's day of salvation, and that it was thought of in Exodus terms. Once more they were to be led out of slavery into a Promised Land—but this time it was to be through the agency of a greater Moses into a better salvation. This thought develops particularly in the inter-Testamental period, and what we have in the Old Testament is merely a hint that such teaching is developing. One thing, however, is clear. The highest Old Testament ideal thinks of salvation in very different terms from national exaltation, and cannot separate it from the salvation of the rest of the world. Yet the main stream of the nation cannot accept this, though still looking forward to God's salvation. The stage is all set for the New Testament.

It is not surprising that after the fall of Jerusalem in A.D. 70, the Jew retained the vision of a return to Palestine. In the Passover ceremony referred to earlier, the Jew still prays, "This year here : next year in Jerusalem". To many pious Jews the establishment of the State of Israel in 1948 seemed, and still seems, the fulfilment of this messianic dream.

GOD THE KING

Thus says the LORD, the God of Israel, "I brought up Israel out of Egypt, and I delivered you from the hand of the Egyptians and from the hand of all the kingdoms that were oppressing you". But you have this day rejected your God, who saves you from all your calamities and your distresses; and you have said, "No! but set a king over us." (1 Sam. 10. 18, 19)

One of the most remarkable things about Israel is the way in which their attitude to kingship differed so completely from that of other nations of the Fertile Crescent. So far as we know, they were the only nation to exist at any time without a king (that is, from the time of Moses to that of Samuel). Even when monarchy had been established, as we have already noted, their idea of the place of the king was quite different. The difference seems to be that essentially Israel thought of themselves as directly under the guidance of Yahweh, expressed through charismatic[6] leaders and prophets, as described, for instance, in the Book of Judges where local leaders such as Deborah (4. 4—5. 31) and Gideon (6. 7—8. 32) are shown as exercising temporary

[6] Under the direct guidance of Yahweh.

GOD THE KING

authority. During this period there was an attempt to institute monarchy by Abimelech (Judges 9), but this was short-lived. The real beginning of the monarchy comes in the time of Samuel (1 Sam. chs. 8—12) under pressure from the Philistines.

The account in these chapters is complicated by the fact that it is composite. One source suggests that the initiative came from Samuel, under the direction of Yahweh (9. 15—10. 1), Saul being accepted by the nation because of his military prowess (ch. 11). The other account, which seems to be later, after experience of kingship, represents Samuel considering the appointment of a king as an act of national apostasy (8. 1-22; 10. 17-27; 12. 1-25). Even in this second account it is clear that the ideal of kingship is that of a man who realizes that he ought to be subject to the will of Yahweh (cf. Deut. 17. 14-20, esp. vv. 18ff). There can, however, be little doubt that at the start the monarchy was thought of particularly as a military leadership. The belief that the institution of kingship was apostasy came after the discovery that even a purely military monarchy was liable to degenerate into the type of kingship known elsewhere, when Israelite kings adopted the "rights" of Canaanite monarchs, and in all probability their cultic functions as well. The adoption of Canaanite ideas of kingship made easier the adoption of Canaanite forms of worship also; and although the exact way in which this happened is not quite clear, there can be little doubt that the monarchy played a large part. It is hardly surprising that later generations without the benefit of accurate historical records looked on the adoption of kingship as the beginning of national apostasy.

Nevertheless, there is abundant evidence to show that at least in theory the king governed by the will of the people, and not by right of divine ancestry or any similar fiction. David, for instance, is invited to reign by representatives of the people (2 Sam. 2. 3, 4; 5. 1-3—note that the relationship of king and people is described as a "covenant"). Solomon, it is true, came to the throne by right of (reputed) nomination by David through a palace *coup d'état*; but it is important to notice that he was not the eldest son, that his accession was at the hands of a prophet of Yahweh, Nathan (1 Kings 1), and there is an implied acceptance of Solomon by the people (1 Kings 1. 39, 40). Any attempt to establish the theory that a man had a right to reign because of his Davidic descent received its death blow, in the Northern Kingdom at any rate, after the death of Solomon. In a most instructive incident (1 Kings 12) Rehoboam went to Shechem to be made king by "all Israel". Instead of the almost automatic confirmation he had expected, this confirmation was refused except on condition that he agreed to a substantial change in the way the monarchy conducted its affairs. On his refusal, the Northern tribes refused to accept him as king, and appointed Jeroboam instead. We also notice the suggestion that Yahweh, in the person of Ahijah the prophet, was behind the division of the kingdoms (1 Kings 11. 29-40). The emphasis on a covenant relationship between king and people receives support in the story of the accession of the infant Jehoash (2 Kings 11. 17), although the fact that it is specifically mentioned here suggests that the custom had fallen into disuse as the Davidic dynasty became established in Judah.

We must also notice particularly the part of the prophets in the making or deposing of a king. It goes back to Samuel, and his making and deposing of Saul, and anointing of David (1 Sam. 15. 17ff; 16. 1ff). We have noted the actions of Nathan and Ahijah, and also remember the part played by Elisha in the deposition of the house of Omri (2 Kings 9). The important part to notice about this story is not that kings could be deposed and replaced by a military usurper—such events were common—but that what happened was done in the name of Yahweh at the instigation of an accepted prophet.

It may, therefore, fairly be said that at least in theory Israel maintains that their ruler is Yahweh, with the king as his vicegerent. The king must rule in accordance with the will of Yahweh (cf. p. ¶¶, above). Yahweh's kingdom is not a territory, but a people, those who accept him and do his will:

> ... if you will obey my voice and keep my covenant, you shall be my own possession among all peoples; for all the earth is mine, and you shall be to me a kingdom of priests and a holy nation. (Ex. 19. 5, 6)

As we should expect, the emphasis on Yahweh as king comes out in worship, and hence especially in psalms. In particular, look at Psalms 93, 95, 96, 97, 98, and 99. The relationship between these psalms and the form of the cultus is disputed, some scholars holding that they are connected with a New Year ceremony in which the king was enthroned as the personification of Yahweh. Whether this be so or not is unimportant in our present context, as the fact remains that Yahweh is seen as the true king of Israel, and not only of Israel but of the whole world. The fact that these psalms were retained and used in the post-exilic period is proof enough that even if they were once connected with such a ceremony, they expressed the understanding of the people about the kingship of Yahweh sufficiently well to be divorced from it without losing their significance.

We may sum up by saying that we cannot separate the kingship of Yahweh from the rest of his nature. Because he is in a covenant relationship with Israel, he must insist on the maintenance of the terms of the covenant. Because he is righteous, he must maintain righteous rule in his kingdom. Because he is the universal God, his kingdom must be a universal kingdom. Because he is saviour and redeemer, his kingdom *will* be established on earth, and men everywhere will be able to come to it.

Nevertheless, the establishment of the kingdom of God is seen by later Old Testament writers in terms of the reign of an ideal human king. This is hardly surprising: temporal rule must be exercised by someone, and in a situation where it might well become necessary to maintain the existence of the kingdom by military power, that "someone" must be able to lead the people of God into battle against the enemies of God. The idea arises, too, from the place of the Davidic dynasty in Judah. In Israel there had been frequent changes of dynasty, usually by military *coup d'état*, but Judah had remained faithful to the house of David. This had given stability to affairs in Judah, and it combined with the belief that the house of David ruled by divine will (cf. 2 Sam. 7. 12-16; Ps. 132. 11, 12) to lead to the expectation that God's salvation would be brought back to Israel through the Davidic line. Moreover, when men looked back to the time of David, it seemed to be a golden age: the boundaries of Israel had been greater than they had ever been since, the kingdoms had been united and strong. David for all his faults, had been strictly loyal to Yahweh, and on the whole his reign had been one of righteousness. Small wonder that when men looked forward to the time of God's salvation, it was seen in terms the rule of a new David:

> Behold the days are coming, says the LORD, when I will raise up for David a righteous Branch, and he shall reign as king and deal wisely, and shall execute justice and righteousness in the land. In his days Judah will be saved, and Israel will dwell securely . . . (Jer. 23. 5, 6)

> I will save my flock, they shall no longer be a prey . . . and I will set up over them one shepherd, my servant David, and he shall feed them . . . And I, the LORD, will be their God, and

my servant David shall be prince among them . . .
(Ezek. 34. 22-4)

Notice also Zech. 12. 7—13. 1, and many references in the Psalms and elsewhere. There is no need to labour the point by multiplying references. The hope of the ideal Davidic king is much more the true Old Testament expectation than is that of a "messiah", which is mainly post-Old Testament. (We may hazard a guess that the emphasis on Messiah rather than a Davidic king may not be unconnected with the experience of the restored monarchy under the Hasmonaeans.) It is the Davidic expectation which forms the centre of Peter's comment on the messiahship of Jesus on the Day of Pentecost (Acts 2. 30, 31), and it is fair to consider it the centre of Old Testament hopes.

GOD THE JUDGE

The concept of Yahweh as Judge is deeply rooted in all parts of the Old Testament. It is not, however, an isolated concept, since it depends entirely on the qualities of God we have already studied. If God is holy in righteousness, then by nature he must be opposed to evil and wrongdoing: if his salvation is for those that fear him and keep his commandments, it follows that when his salvation is manifested, his condemnation also is shown on those that reject him and do not follow his ways. The mercy of God does not imply a sloppy sentimental nature that will overlook evil. "He's a good fellow, and 'twill all be well" represents the easy optimism of those who have not understood the nature of the Holy One of Israel. "Holy Love" insists that the unholy are cut off from love. If the quality of *chesed* means that God will maintain his covenant with those who keep it, his steadfastness also means that those who do not keep it will be cut off. This is severe, and if it were the whole story we might well say, "Who may abide it?" As we know, it is precisely this dilemma which St Paul saw as the failure of Judaism, and from which we are saved by Christ. But he does not save us by contradicting the Old Testament understanding of God, but by reforming the nature of man. Here again, the Old Testament finds its consummation in the New Testament.

With this in mind, we may now consider the words used in the Old Testament. The verb is *shaphat*, and closely connected with it is the noun *mishpat*, usually translated "judgement", and its active participle *shophet*, "a judge". In one or two places we also find *din*, which means more particularly strict retributive justice, although it is commonly used by Jews to-day in connection with the administration of the law.[7] *Mishpat* on the other hand is best seen as "the verdict of the court" in a particular case, the equivalent of our verdicts of "guilty" or "not guilty": or it may be somewhat the equivalent of our case law, that is, a statement of the law in a particular case which may then be applied in similar cases later. Since justice is particularly the king's justice, *mishpat* also comes to mean the promulgated statement of the will of the king. In particular, it is God who gives *mishpat*, and to walk in his judgements is to keep his ways:

> Then I said, "These are only the poor, they have no sense;
>   for they do not know the way of the LORD,
>   the law (*mishpat*) of their God.
> I will go to the great,
>   and will speak to them;
> for they know the way of the LORD,
>   the law (*mishpat*) of their God.   (Jer. 5. 4, 5)

To keep *mishpat* is to do righteousness:

---

[7] The *Beth Din* is simply the "house of judgement", or better "the place where disputes are settled and justice administered".

GOD THE JUDGE

> Yet they seek me daily,
>   and delight to know my ways,
> as if they were a nation that did righteousness (*tsedaqah*)
>   and did not forsake the ordinance (*mishpat*) of their God;
> they ask of me righteous judgements (*mishpatim*),
>   they delight to draw near to God.   (Isa. 58. 2)

and is specifically applied to the contents of the *Torah*:

> Hear, O Israel, the statutes and the ordinances (*mishpatim*) which I speak in your hearing this day, and you shall learn them . . .   (Deut. 5. 1)

Remembering the meaning of *Torah* (see p. 28), it is clear that where *mishpat* comes from God, it has the meaning of the "will of God" or the "way of God", as for instance in Isa. 42. 4, referring to the Servant of the Lord:

> He will not fail or be discouraged
>   till he has established justice (*mishpat*) in the earth;
>   and the coastlands wait for his law.

God's judgement is not capricious or unpredictable. It is his way of life, given to Israel and completely derived from his inner nature. If Israel truly knows Yahweh, they will know his *mishpat*; if they keep it, when they stand before the judge they may be certain that he will give righteous *mishpat*, the verdict of "innocent". If, on the other hand they have failed to keep *mishpat* then the right (and therefore righteous) verdict will be "guilty".

The function of Yahweh as judge is, of course, closely connected with his being king, for one of the main functions of the king is to administer justice (cf. 2 Sam. 15. 1-6):

> Say among the nations, "The LORD reigns! [i.e., Yahweh has become king]
>   Yea, the world is established, it shall never be moved;
>   he will judge the peoples with equity."   (Ps. 96. 10)

Here it is clear that "judge" means not merely the act of judgement, but more particularly the giving of *mishpat* so that people may live by it. When we think of God as judge, it is important to remember that he is not only the law-enforcer, but also, and perhaps primarily, the one who first makes known his way so that it may be followed.

Nevertheless, the enforcement of his way is important, and it is clear from many stories in the Old Testament that Yahweh was considered to be a continual judge with his people. Wherever men transgress his commandment, he is there, active to put things right. This applies to kings (cf. 1 Sam. 15. 24-6), to individuals (Isa. 1. 27, 28) and to Israel as a whole (Jer. 11. 9-11). Ideas such as this lead to the belief in a final Day of Judgement. We have already noticed (pp. 24-5, 33, above) how Amos insists that the Day of Yahweh will be a day of judgement, and this emphasis on God's visitation of his people is characteristic of all the prophets. Indeed the verb "visit" implies "visit in judgement" or "punish" in many places. In the prophets, it is clear that this visitation will begin with Israel. It is in the apocalyptic literature, developing for the most part in the post-Old Testament period, that we find the idea that Israel, the righteous nation, will be judged by exaltation over others. This idea is found in Daniel 7. 22 :

> ... until the Ancient of Days came, and judgement (*din*) was given for the saints of the Most High, and the time came when the saints received the kingdom ...

but it is a degeneration. The clear Biblical message is that the judgement of God will, and does, begin with the people of God, who have two inescapable duties : to walk in his ways, and to make those ways known to the rest of mankind. Failure to fulfil these will result in judgement. When it comes to other nations, they will be judged either because they have refused to listen to the word of Yahweh when they had the opportunity, or because they failed to follow the ordinary dictates of the natural law which they ought to have known anyway. Any other concept would violate the holy justice of God.

THE GOD OF HISTORY

All that has been said so far makes it clear that there can be no suggestion that the Hebrews ever considered God as a sort of "absentee landlord", with no concern for what was happening in the world of men. Their whole national history, as interpreted by the prophets, disposed of any such idea completely. When we speak of the "God of History", we imply that God has a purpose which he is bringing to fruition through the way in which men and nations are living together. Nothing that happens is outside his control; everything has its place in his pattern. It might seem that this is a deterministic concept: God is in control of everything, man can do nothing. But it has to be taken alongside the equally sure conviction that man has freewill, can oppose the will of God, and can fight against him. This is the whole philosophical and religious problem of predestination and freewill, and the Old Testament does not even attempt to solve it. The Hebrews were not a philosophical race: their religion was practical and pragmatic. They *knew* that God was active in history: they had experienced his mighty acts both in salvation and in judgement. They knew also that man was capable both of following the way of God and of departing from it, and that he did both by his own free choice. They did not try to reconcile these opposites: they lived by them. It has to be said, however, that in spite of the Exodus tradition, it took time for the Hebrews to grasp completely its implications and to understand that God was in control of the affairs of other nations as well as of their own.

The belief in Yahweh as God of history develops precisely parallel to that in Yahweh as a universal God. For

Amos, God was concerned with the way in which the Syrians had come to their land and the Philistines had come from Crete (9. 7). Isaiah sees that the military successes of the Assyrians are at the behest of Yahweh, and that when they have fulfilled his purposes they will themselves have to answer for their misdeeds (10. 5-19) Nahum realizes that the doom of Nineveh is brought about by Yahweh just because of these misdeeds (2. 13—3. 4). Jeremiah sees the vision of the cauldron, meaning that Yahweh is calling the tribes of the north against Jerusalem (1. 13-16), and teaches that the conquest of the city by the Babylonians is part of Yahweh's visitation (32. 1-5). Deutero-Isaiah boldly asserts that Cyrus, the conqueror of Babylonia, is the instrument of Yahweh, and that the purpose of his campaigns is to be found in the fate of Israel: Cyrus indeed is Yahweh's anointed (Isa. 45. 1-7). Examples could be multiplied tenfold.

In considering Yahweh in this way, it is logical to go on to consider the end of history, that is, the time when his will will be established on earth. Naturally, the prophets see this in terms of the fulfilment of their own particular epoch, in each case with the restoration of Israel (cf. Isa. 10. 24-7, Jer. 29. 10-14), and the Second Isaiah has the main theme that the time of fulfilment of God's purposes has now arrived. When, therefore, we look at later writings, we are not surprised to find that they divide time into two ages— this age, and the age to come—and that the idea of the fulfilment of history is linked with ideas of judgement and of the Davidic and Messianic hopes. This is found in various ways in the inter-Testamental writers, but in each case the theme is the same—that this age will be brought to an end by the intervention of God himself, in many cases using the messiah as an instrument, who will justify the righteous and punish the wicked, and will set up a reign of righteousness and peace on earth under a Davidic king. In this reign, Israel will be the priestly nation for all the peoples of the world, who will then know and worship Yahweh. But this is not the end of the world as that phrase is commonly understood: it is better described as the "consummation of the age", an end of the present order, and a fresh start, almost a new creation.

THE GOD OF NATURE AND CREATION

And she did not know
   that it was I who gave her
   the grain, the wine, and the oil,
and who lavished upon her silver
   and gold which they used for Baal.   (Hos. 2. 8)

It seems obvious to us that if we believe in God at all, it can only be in a God who created and sustains the universe. To try to divorce God from creation seems impossible. This, however, is only so if we are monotheists. As we have seen, although monotheistic faith was implicit from the Exodus onwards it took a long time to come to fruition; and during the period between the settlement and the exile many, if not most, Israelites were for all practical purposes polytheists. It is worth thinking briefly how this happened.

Yahweh was made known to the Israelites through his mighty acts in Egypt and in the desert. He was a God who overcame their enemies, led them through the desert, and made himself known in the storm, fire, and earthquake. When the Israelites entered Canaan, they came into contact with a quite different form of religion, directed towards the maintenance of an agricultural way of life. No doubt the strict Israelite would have felt that Yahweh's prowess in bringing them into Canaan showed that he was stronger and better than the Canaanite gods, and we might expect the same sort of process to take place as often did happen in the ancient world, the religion of the invader becoming the new religion of the land. Later ages certainly believed that this *ought* to have happened, and the account of the practical extermination of the Canaanites found in Josh. 10. 40 quite clearly reflects the comment of a later writer. The reality was quite different. The traditions found in Judges 1. 16-36 and Josh. 13—17 (e.g. 13. 13; 16. 10; 17. 13) show that the invaders settled down alongside the earlier inhabitants, in many cases using them as slaves. Let us consider what would have been in the mind of an Israelite peasant who had taken over the farm of a Canaanite. He had probably kept on either the previous owners, or other Canaanites, as slaves or hired hands. In the nature of the case he would be largely dependent upon them so far as methods of cultivation were concerned, and it would be as much to their advantage as to his to make sure that the land was fruitful. If the crop failed, the slave would starve before the farmer, if indeed he was not put to death for sabotage. Now the Canaanites knew that in the past fertility had been ensured by going through the prescribed rituals of their own gods; the method had not failed in the past, and they would no doubt urge the new owner to do the same. What would his reactions be? Yahweh had certainly conquered: he had showed that he was a better warrior, he had led them through the desert; but what did he know about agriculture? It would be against human nature if a majority, if not all, did not take out an insurance policy. Yahweh was certainly God of Israel, and they would continue to worship him. But the local gods certainly had more experience at this business of growing crops than Yahweh, and it would have been the height of folly not to worship them as well. So we find a sort of dual religion growing up, in which Yahweh was worshipped and invoked in matters concerning him, notably matters of war and battle, while the *baʿalim* were worshipped in their sphere.

This process may be seen at work in Judges. The frame-

THE GOD OF NATURE AND CREATION

work and historical philosophy of the book is admittedly late, and affected by Deuteronomic ideas, but there can be little doubt that the summary contained in 2. 11-19 is a fair reflection of the facts: when the people were at peace they worshipped the *ba'alim*; when oppressed, they quite naturally turned to Yahweh, god of armies and battles. The influence of Deuteronomy is seen not in the facts themselves, but in the way they are presented, and in the underlying intrepretation that it was because of their apostasy that Yahweh sent their enemies. We may very much doubt whether the people of the time would have seen it that way at all.

It is sometimes suggested that a process of syncretism took place, as a result of which Yahweh was worshipped by Israel on the high places (the sacred spots inherited from the Canaanites) with the rituals and beliefs of ba'alism. This seems improbable. Had it been so to any great extent, the frequent remonstrances of the prophets against the worship of the local gods instead of Yahweh would have been meaningless, and the quotation from Hosea at the head of this section would have been pointless, for such syncretism would have meant that they *did* believe that it was Yahweh who gave them the grain, the wine, and the oil. Rather, as we have said, we see the fusion of two systems, both continuing side by side. The process of accepting other gods into Israel seems to have been hastened during the reign of Solomon by the acceptance of foreign deities into the Jerusalem cultus. According to 1 Kings 11. 1-8 this was at the instance of his foreign wives, though we may doubt whether this was the real reason. In all probability both foreign wives and foreign gods were results of his general foreign policy. An alliance with a foreign nation implies an alliance of the two cults as well: if the gods are allied, they will clearly be worshipped together. Trade agreements and military pacts were frequently sealed by royal marriages, and there can be little doubt that these foreign princesses would continue to take part in the newly established cultus of their own nation. But we can hardly believe that it was simply to satisfy the women of his harem that Solomon departed so radically from the native tradition. In the Northern Kingdom we can see a similar process at work with the introduction of the Tyrian cultus after the marriage of Ahab and Jezebel. (It is important to notice that the work of Elijah is the rooting out, not of "native" ba'alism, but of the cult of a foreign god.

In the same way that belief in Yahweh as God of nature is not found in the early days, we find that belief in him as creator is also absent. It is true that the reason given in the Exodus decalogue for the keeping of the Sabbath is that it is a memorial of the end of creation (20. 11), but we notice that the Deuteronomic version (5. 12-15) gives the quite different reason that it is a rest for master and slave in which they are to remember the national bondage in Egypt, the Sabbath being a weekly memorial of their deliverance. It is difficult to say for certain that either is original to the time of Moses, but there can be little doubt that the "Exodus" reason is far earlier than the "Creation" reason. In all probability we have here two commentaries on the Sabbath, one Deuteronomic and the other exilic or post-exilic, possibly connected with P. The earliest creation story in the Bible is that of J (Genesis 2. 4ff) and here the attribution of creation to Yahweh is very much less pointed than in the later story of Gen. 1. 1—2. 4a. Indeed in the J narrative the mention of creation seems little more than a prelude to its real interests, the nature of man and woman, the beginning of sin, and the causes of man's discomfort on the earth. The fact that it is stated shows that it was at least beginning to be accepted in Israel, but the manner of its stating shows that it comes in almost incidentally.

THE GOD OF NATURE AND CREATION

Israelite man is starting to ask questions about himself and his relation to the world in which he finds himself, and he has to relate the answers to God. He realizes the universality of the difficulties which he is trying to explain, and sees that they must go back to the beginning of things. Being also sure that nothing happens without the agency of God, he finds himself committed to a doctrine of creation by Yahweh. But it is certain that a Moabite dealing with the same material would have come to the conclusion that creation was by Chemosh; and had the author of J known of this it seems doubtful whether he would have seen it as incongruous. He was used to a situation in which Yahweh and other gods were worshipped together, with many functions overlapping. This would have been simply another example.

As we should expect, it is the prophets who start to bring these doctrines to full light. In Amos there are two passages (4. 13 and 5. 8, 9) which suggest Yahweh as creator, but both are suspect, since neither really "fits" its present context, and it is difficult to believe that Israel at that time had got as far as thinking of Yahweh as all-sovereign creator. As Hosea shows, they had not even reached the stage of believing him to be responsible for the growth of the crops on which their life depended; only after this had been accepted would it have been possible to move on to a full doctrine of creation (see Hos. 2. 1-17), and this has to wait until ba'alism has been fully rooted out.

There was a shortlived attempt at reform under Hezekiah (2 Kings 18. 1-5), which may have been influenced by the prophetic teaching, although almost certainly also influenced by political considerations, being a purge of the Assyrian worship introduced by Ahaz (2 Kings 16. 10ff) when Hezekiah revolted. The insistence on the need to root out the Canaanite cultus found in Deuteronomy seems to have been behind the reforms of Josiah (cf. Deut. 12. 1-4, 29-31; 18. 9ff, etc., with 2 Kings 23), although even here political considerations are probably not entirely absent. Even this reform, far-reaching as it was, was reversed by his successors (2 Kings 23. 37), and the hold that the older practices had on the people is amply attested by both Jeremiah and Ezekiel (see Jer. 44. 15ff, Ezek. 8 and many other references).

It was the exile in Babylonia which really settled matters. There can be little doubt that the period of captivity led to the apostasy of those whose real sympathies were with the agricultural religions of the area, and also to the strengthening of the faith in Yahweh of those who looked to the God of Israel. The work of the prophets in the previous two centuries had made much clearer the nature of the choice to be made. The teachings of Jeremiah and Ezekiel on the place and responsibility of the individual (see pp. 123-6, below) and of Deutero-Isaiah on monotheism make the issues quite clear, and allow the individual to make a choice apart from the nation as a whole. The result is that in the post-exilic literature there is never any suggestion of a reversion to ba'alism. The worship of Yahweh may be neglected or performed in a slovenly way, but it is still Yahweh who is being worshipped. The next threat, when it came, was not from ba'alism but from Hellenism, and was a very different matter.

It is only when it is seen that God is in control in the cosmos that a real doctrine of creation becomes possible. At first sight, it is surprising that so little is found in the Old Testament on this subject. Apart from a few isolated references, the material is contained in about half a dozen chapters: Gen. 1 and 2; Job 38—41; Prov. 8. 1-31; and a few Psalms, 8, 19, 33, 95, 104, 136, 148, with a few odd references in others. The key to this is found in Psalm 136, which is mainly concerned with the mighty works of the Exodus; the praise of creation is much more in the nature of a prologue to the rest of the Psalm. This is the way the

THE GOD OF NATURE AND CREATION 61

Israelite thought of creation: it happened, certainly, and Yahweh was responsible. But it is more important to know Yahweh in what he has done and what he is doing now. What happened at the beginning is a philosophical rather than a practical question, and as such has very little interest for the Hebrews.

With these ideas in mind, we may look at the passages mentioned. The most important is the P account in Gen. 1. 1—2. 4a. We must remember that it does not stand alone; Assyria and Babylonia had their creation stories as well, and the Genesis account shows similarities and affinities in a number of ways. Indeed, it looks as if the Priestly writer took over already existing and well-known material, and reshaped and rewrote it to bring out his own particular teachings. In order to get at its particular views, therefore, it is necessary, not to make a complete analysis, but to see the differences between it and the rock from which it was hewed. We may notice, of course, the background assumptions which he takes over, but these will not help us to understand the specifically Jewish insights and doctrines.

The first and most obvious point is that while the Babylonian story tells of conflicts between the various gods and goddesses, ending in the death of one of them and the creation of the world from her body, the Hebrew account is absolutely monotheistic. God is supreme, and all that happens is by his deliberate will: when creation is finished, he sees that it is all "very good" (1. 31). It is difficult to overstress the importance of this. For the Jew, God is completely in control in a good creation. That this raises enormous problems cannot be denied, problems which never arise in a polytheistic or dualistic religion. The greatest is the problem of the existence of suffering and evil. Polytheism has no difficulty in postulating conflict between the gods, in which men are mere pawns, especially as morality is rarely one of the qualities attributed to such deities.

Dualism postulates two eternal principles, one good, one evil, with this world as their battlefield. Such solutions are impossible in a monotheism, and we shall see later how the Hebrew grapples with them. But besides raising problems, this belief also leads to *hope*. In such a creation God's purposes are being worked out, and "all manner of things shall be well". Moreover, in such a consistent creation, with such a consistent God, man must conform himself, or fall under the wrath of God. The very nature of Judaism, therefore, leads to this understanding of creation, and to no other.

The second thing to notice is that creation itself is subject to God, and is part of his purpose. This implies two things: first, that man is not ruled by creation, as would be the case were we to accept the teachings of those who practise astrology; secondly, that hope extends to the whole of creation. So we get the messianic verses in Isa. 11. 6-9, and find St Paul, in a thoroughly Hebraic passage, insisting that "the whole creation has been groaning in travail together until now", waiting for the time when "the creation itself will be set free from its bondage to decay and obtain the glorious liberty of the children of God" (Rom. 8. 21, 22).

Finally, we notice the place of man in creation. He is made in the "image of God". We are not to take this literally, implying that in his physical shape man is a copy of a supernatural being. It quite clearly has reference to his moral and psychical qualities. Exactly what is meant by the "image of God", and its relationship to the state of man after the "Fall" is one of those matters debated endlessly by certain schools of systematic theologians; it is not debated by the Old Testament, which is content to accept the fact that human nature is basically good, and has a definite affinity with the divine nature. Even this is not argued, nor explicitly stated; it is the background to all Old Testament

THE GOD OF NATURE AND CREATION 63

thought about the nature of man. It is perfectly expressed in Ps. 8. 3-8 :

> When I look at thy heavens, the work of thy fingers,
> the moon and the stars which thou hast established;
> What is man that thou are mindful of him,
> and the son of man that thou dost care for him?
> Yet thou hast made him little less than God,
> and dost crown him with glory and honour.
> Thou hast given him dominion over the works of thy hands;
> thou hast put all things under his feet . . .

Whatever we may think of the "Fall" story in Gen. 3, it is certain that the Old Testament gives no support to those systems of theology which look on man as "totally depraved". Sinful he may be, in revolt against God, but the Hebrew knows that human nature is not depraved but dignified, made in the image of God.

When we come to consider the background ideas of creation, one stands out : the creation described in Gen. 1 is not absolute creation but the giving of form to previously existing matter. As has been stressed, philosophy was not a Hebrew failing at all. For the Hebrew, all that mattered was that everything was as it was because Yahweh willed it so. He was not interested in the "How?" of creation : to go behind the empirical facts he knew was a pointless exercise in academic thinking.

We may put it another way by saying that creation was always seen in relation to man, never in the abstract. This is particularly noticeable in Gen. 2 (J), in which man is really the first of creation, trees, animals, and woman being created for him. The description of creation in Job 38—41 is not intended to help Job understand it : on the contrary, it is to show that Job *cannot* understand. And if he cannot understand creation, how will it be possible for him to understand the mind of the creator? How dare he question the ways of God? In Ps. 19 we have the description of the way in which God created the sun and the heavenly host—but the point is made simply to illustrate the way in which the *torah* was given to Israel, and there can be little doubt that for the Psalmist *torah* was the more important. Psalm 33 mentions creation, but simply to lead on to the essentially practical assertion that because Yahweh has done this, he is in control of his earth and is guiding its history, and that true salvation is to be found not in military might but in that sure trust in Yahweh which is (or ought to be) the glory of his Chosen People. Similar comments might be made in every case.

We also notice that in Gen. 1 the creative act was the speaking of the word: "God said . . . and there was . . ." Once his will has been expressed, the fact exists. A similar point is made in Ps. 33. 6. Creation, then, can only express the nature of God. To quote St Paul again, "Ever since the creation of the world his invisible nature, namely his eternal power and deity, has been clearly perceived in the things that have been made" (Rom. 1. 20). The Old Testament has little support for those who would deny Natural Theology! This comes out in another way in our final passage, Prov. 8. 22-31. Wisdom, personified, is saying that she is the very first-made of all creation, and that

. . . when he marked out the foundations of the earth,
then I was beside him, like a master workman . . .

(Prov. 8. 29, 30)

Wisdom, the expression of the nature of God, his first-made, is the co-workman of God in the act of creation.[8] As a corollary, men are able, through the wisdom given by God, to understand him and the world in which they live, so as

[8] It is possible that the correct translation is not "master workman" but "little child" (cf. the margin of the R.S.V.), and this would fit the following lines rather better. But the point remains the same, that wisdom is a reflection of the nature of God, and through wisdom, men may come to understand his ways.

"TO WHOM THEN WILL YOU LIKEN GOD?" 65

to walk in the ways of God, ways which are rooted in his nature, and have been so since the beginning.

"TO WHOM THEN WILL YOU LIKEN GOD?"

The second of the "Ten Words" expressly forbids the making of any graven image for worship, and the clear implication is that this includes any representation of Yahweh. Nevertheless, the story related in Ex. 32 shows that even then the people were quite willing to worship Yahweh in the form of a bull,[9] even though the story has probably been subject to later revision, and the use of bull images in the worship of Yahweh is seen to go back to the earliest days of the nation. Recent evidence from Assyria suggests, however, that the use of animal forms may not be intended as direct representation, but that the animals are to be thought of as mounts on which the unseen god is riding. In the minds of a few this may well have been so, but there can be little doubt that to the great majority, the bull was Yahweh.

There were other cult objects dating from the Exodus period also, the serpent and the ark, both connected with Jerusalem in the same way that the bull was connected with the Northern sanctuaries. The serpent is first mentioned in Num. 21. 6-9, where it appears as a prophylactic charm: the word *saraph* used in this context may well be connected with the seraphim seen as attendants of Yahweh in Isa. 6. It is by no means impossible that what started originally as an image of Yahweh became thought of as the image of one

[9] Is the story a genuine reminiscence of desert days, in which case the setting up of bull images by Jeroboam (1 Kings 12. 28-30) is the continuing of a genuine tradition? Or is it a story told in order to provide Aaronic sanction for this action? Probably the former, revised by Northern scribes, and revised again under the influence of Deuteronomy by Southern scribes of the exilic or immediate pre-exilic period.

of his attendants: it is also possible that the seraphim were originally considered as mounts of Yahweh, as we suggested above with regard to the bull. We hear no more of this object until its removal by Hezekiah (2 Kings 18. 4), though it is clear that it had been retained in the Temple and used for cultic purposes.

Far more important is the ark. That the presence of God was thought to accompany the ark there can be little doubt:

> And whenever the ark set out, Moses said, "Arise, O LORD, and let thy enemies be scattered . . ." and when it rested, he said, "Return, O LORD, to the ten thousand thousands of Israel".
> (Num. 10. 35,36)

At the battle of Ebenezer, after the initial defeat, the ark was brought from Shiloh to the battlefield,

> . . . and when they learned that the ark of the LORD had come to the camp, the Philistines were afraid; or they said, "The gods have come into the camp." (1 Sam. 4. 6, 7)

The word here translated "the gods" is *'elohim*, the ordinary word for God, and since the Hebrew has no article, that is almost certainly the meaning here. After the final defeat, Phineas' wife names her child Ichabod ("no glory") for

> . . . she said, "The glory has departed from Israel, for the ark of God has been captured." (1 Sam. 4. 22)

When the ark was brought to Jerusalem, there can be no doubt that it was believed that so the presence of God was brought into the city:

> As the ark of the LORD came into the city of David, Michal the daughter of Saul looked out of the window, and saw King David leaping and dancing before the LORD. (2 Sam. 6. 16)

We also notice that when the Temple had been completed by Solomon the priests

"TO WHOM THEN WILL YOU LIKEN GOD?" 67

> brought the ark of the covenant of the LORD to its place ...
> underneath the wings of the cherubim.   (1 Kings 8. 6)

and we remember that the cherubim were considered the throne of Yahweh (Ps. 80. 1; 99. 1). The ark seems to have been an oblong box of acacia wood, about four feet long and two feet square in cross-section (Ex. 25. 10). The ancient tradition (Deut. 10. 2; 1 Kings 8. 9) is that it contained the two tables of the law given on Mount Sinai.[10] The probability is that it contained stones from Mount Sinai, intended to provide a dwelling place for the God whose original home was at Sinai (in exactly the same way that Naaman required some of the soil of Israel on which to worship Israel's God, 2 Kings 5. 17).

After being brought to the Temple, the ark disappears from mention. In all probability it was among the treasures carried off by Nebuchadrezzar. So far as is known, there was no substitute for it in the second Temple, though there was the "mercy seat" which, according to P (Ex. 25. 17-22) was closely connected with the ark, and provided the meeting place between God and his people. The cherubim on the mercy seat also seem closely related to the cherubim mentioned in connection with the ark.

Mention of Mount Sinai leads us on to think about ideas held about an earthly home of Yahweh. There can be little doubt that in the earliest traditions Sinai (or Horeb: the two names seem interchangeable) is thought of as the place where men go to worship. It seems, too, that Sinai was thought of as the home of Yahweh, from whence he came to succour his people, and where he could be met. Elijah goes to Horeb to find him (1 Kings 19. 1-18); Moses first meets with Yahweh on Sinai (Ex. 3. 1—4. 17) and is told that this is the place where the people are to worship. It is

---

[10] The tradition mentioned in Heb. 9. 4 of the pot of manna and Aaron's rod seem to be based on no early evidence.

the place where the covenant is made, and where God is stated to descend to earth. We find, too, that the city of Jerusalem and the Temple in particular were thought of as a second dwelling place, and it is probable that this is connected with the presence of the ark (cf. Amos 1. 2; Ps. 132. 5, 13; 135. 21). Nevertheless, as the story of Elijah going to Horeb shows, this was not thought of as a permanent change of location, but rather as a sort of "town house" which he could use to be amongst his people.

Yet alongside this primitive concept there were from the beginning elements in Israelite thought that considered God as not bound to any earthly location. The story of the giving of the Ten Words shows Yahweh as *coming down* to Sinai (Ex. 19. 18), while that of the Tower of Babel (Gen. 11. 1-9) shows God as being aware of what was happening in the land of the two rivers, and of his going to visit men there. Jacob at Bethel (Gen. 28. 10-22) considered that place to be "the house of God" and the "gate of heaven"—the idea clearly being that the real dwelling place of God was heaven, and that he was made known at his sanctuaries. Similar stories of theophanies were no doubt told at all the sanctuaries, but the point is not that he could be met there, but that his presence showed the sanctuary to be an extension of his heavenly dwelling. Quite clearly, as the universality of God becomes accepted, ideas of earthly dwellings fall into the background, and the heavenly abode of Yahweh becomes generally current thought. Nevertheless, Jerusalem is still thought to remain in a special sense the home of God:

> Thus says the LORD: I will return to Zion, and will dwell in the midst of Jerusalem, and Jerusalem shall be called the faithful city, and the mountain of the LORD of hosts . . .
>
> (Zech. 8. 3)

and a similar idea comes out in Solomon's dedication of the Temple in 1 Kings 8. 27-30, a passage which owes its

"TO WHOM THEN WILL YOU LIKEN GOD?" 69

present form very much to Deuteronomic influence. The mode of God's presence in the Temple we shall look at again when we discuss the *shekinah* (p. 75, below).

Particularly in the earlier strata of the Old Testament, there are many passages which suggest that it was not impossible, indeed not unusual, for men to meet Yahweh in their daily doings. In many of these passages later redactors have substituted that appearance of the "angel of Yahweh" for the appearance of Yahweh himself, but in most cases sufficient traces of the original story remain to show that it was originally told of a theophany. Manoah in Judges 13 is reported to have been given a message by the angel of the Lord, but in v. 22 his response is, "We shall surely die, for we have seen God". A similar passage occurs in Gen. 16. 7-13, while a definite theophany to Abraham appears in 17. 1-22. In the Burning Bush episode (Ex. 3), it is stated in v. 2 that the vision was that of the angel of the Lord, whereas the rest of the story makes it clear that this again was a divine manifestation. Examples such as these make it quite clear that the term "the angel of the Lord" is often used as a convenient periphrasis for the appearance of Yahweh himself. It is not for us to judge, of course, whether those reporting theophanies of this kind were trying to put into words a spiritual experience, or whether we have stories of messengers of God who found themselves treated as God himself. The important point is that God was believed to be able to appear in this way.[11]

---

[11] We need to remember that our modern ideas of angels as pretty-pretty creatures with fairy wings, etc., have no basis whatsoever in Scripture. An angel is God's messenger, and we have only to read the account of what happened to the angels at Sodom (Gen. 19) to realize that their form was most definitely human! In later times the growing belief in the transcendence of God led to the growth of a parallel belief that God communicated with men by means of spiritual beings: and under Persian influences, ideas of an angelic hierarchy developed. In the earlier period in all

In a very large number of places expressions are used in the Old Testament about God which seem to attribute to him human characteristics. He is reputed to have arms, eyes, ears, and other parts of the body, and his ways are often described in very human terms. It is important to realize that the use of anthropomorphic terms does not necessarily mean that the people who used them really thought of God as a "super-man". It is simply an illustration of the inadequacy of language to express ideas except in terms derived from human experience.[12] With this warning, we must note that in some parts of the Bible phraseology is used which leads us to believe that some at least thought of God as able to walk the earth in quasi-human form. The story of the Garden of Eden in Genesis 3 is a good example, and there is a good deal of similar material in J. But this way of thinking drops out very quickly, and unless we have good reason to think that God is being literally described in human terms, we shall be well advised to think of anthropomorphism as being much more in the nature of metaphor.

To sum up, it is clear that though the Hebrews thought of a generalized presence of God, they thought also of a more localized presence in special circumstances, either in a

probability any prophet or seer who claimed to speak in the name of the Lord was thought of as a messenger (angel) of Yahweh. It is worth looking at stories of theophanies and trying to see which are reports of spirtual experiences and which accounts of messages given by human "angels".

[12] We shall see later that the Hebrew would have drawn no distinction between the psychical function and the organ which carried it out; they would not divorce, e.g., the abstract sense of sight from the physical eyes, so that when they wanted to say that God would have no dealings with sin, they said, "Thou that art of purer eyes than to behold evil". An examination of language used to-day to describe God will show that though it has a more philosophical flavour, it is still using terms derived from experience, simply because language can express nothing else.

particular sanctuary, or for a particular purpose connected with selected individuals. Such ideas seem to lie behind the vision described in Ezek. 1. He certainly describes the vision of Yahweh in human terms :

> ... seated above the likeness of a throne was a likeness as it were of a human form.   (Ezek. 1. 26)

but it is made quite clear that he does not intend us to think that Yahweh was *really* like that

> Such was the appearance of the likeness of the glory of the LORD.   (Ezek. 1. 28)

The description is intended to convey an impression of a being quite indescribable and totally different from man, with the attribute of enormous speed, so that while he is here, he can be anywhere more quickly than lightning, and cannot be confined by any earthly barriers. Similarly, in the vision of the restored Temple, the Glory of Yahweh is seen coming to the Temple from the East (Ezek. 43. 1-4). But we notice that there is no idea of the omnipresence of God in any abstract way. Yahweh is to be found particularly where his people are found, and especially in his Temple when it is standing, and when his people are in their own land.

This is seen particularly in the twin concepts of the "name" and the "glory". For the man of the Old Testament, the name was not simply a convenient means of distinguishing one person from another : it was an integral part of that person. This is seen in the way in which men are given names which particularly fit their characters, or the parts they have to play in God's providence (cf. Gen. 17. 5, 6). It was commonly believed that to know the name of a person was to have power over him (since one now possessed a part of him) (cf. Gen. 32. 22-32). So, when it is said that God will choose a place to "make his name dwell there" (Deut. 12. 11), the implication is that he himself will dwell there. After the priests have blessed Israel, it is said that they have "put my name" upon the people (Num. 6. 27), that is, they have conveyed to the people God's power and presence. The name of God, therefore, is almost equivalent to a synonym for the "nature" of God.

In the same way, "glory" means far more in the Old Testament than it does in common speech to-day. Indeed, in rendering two Hebrew words, *kabod* and *hebel*, as "glory" and "vanity" respectively, we are really perverting their meaning. For us these two are very close in meaning, both having reference to outward show and appearance. In Hebrew, however, *hebel*, with its basic significance of "breath" or "vapour", comes to mean something worthless, useless, unsubstantial, without significance, whereas *kabod* comes from a root meaning "to be heavy", and refers to those things that are real, substantial, and meaningful:

> Men of low estate are but a breath (*hebel*),
>   men of high estate are a delusion;
> in the balances they go up;
>   they are altogether lighter than a breath (*hebel*, R.V. lighter than vanity). (Ps. 62. 9)

This may be contrasted with the description of the righteous man in Psalm 112, which concludes (v. 9):

> His righteousness endures for ever;
>   his horn is exalted in honour (*kabod*).

So *kabod* comes to mean "the reality of a person". For instance:

> My heart is steadfast, O God,
>   my heart is steadfast!
> I will sing and make melody!
>   Awake, my soul (*kabod*)! (Ps. 57. 7, 8)

where quite clearly it is used as equivalent to "myself". It is used in parallel to *nephesh*, "soul" (see pp. 78f below) in Genesis 49. 6 :

> O my soul, come not into their council;
> O my spirit (*kabod*), be not joined to their company.

When the word comes to be applied to God, since his inward nature is known only as he reveals it, "glory" may be defined as "God's nature revealed to his people". It is impossible to go into its full use here, but we must look at a few passages. After the events on Mt Sinai, Moses asks Yahweh,

> "I pray thee, show me thy glory". (Ex. 33. 18)

and as the following verses show, the showing of the glory was a theophany described in very anthropomorphic terms. It is, however, more usual to find the glory of God in natural phenomena, especially the volcano and the thunderstorm (cf. Ex. 24. 15-17; Ps. 29. 1-3, 5-9).

The glory of Yahweh is, however, particularly manifested, as we would expect, in his mighty acts :

> ... as I live, and as all the earth shall be filled with the glory of the LORD, none of the men who have seen my glory and my signs which I wrought in Egypt ... shall see the land which I swore to give to their fathers ... (Num. 14. 21-3)

We should also expect the glory to be closely connected with righteousness, holiness and kingship :

> The LORD reigns; let the earth rejoice;
>   let the many coastlands be glad!
> Clouds and thick darkness are round about him;
>   righteousness and justice are the foundation of his throne.
> Fire goes before him,
>   and burns up his adversaries round about.
> His lightnings lighten the world;
>   the earth sees and trembles ...
> The heavens proclaim his righteousness;
>   and all the peoples behold his glory. (Ps. 97. 1-4, 6)

where the "violent" natural concept of "glory" is taken up into the ethical. The classic example of the combination of "holiness" and "glory" is, of course, the vision of Isaiah (Isa. 6. 3):

> Holy, holy, holy is the LORD of hosts;
> the whole earth is full of his glory.

followed by Isaiah's insight into his own moral unworthiness.

Finally, the glory of God is connected with salvation, both for righteous individuals:

> Surely his salvation is at hand for those who fear him,
> that glory may dwell in our land.
> Steadfast love (*chesed*) and faithfulness will meet;
> righteousness (*tsedeq*) and peace will kiss each other.
> (Ps. 85. 9, 10)

and for the nation:

> Arise, shine; for your light has come,
> and the glory of the LORD has risen upon you.
> For behold, darkness shall cover the earth,
> and thick darkness the peoples;
> but the LORD will arise upon you,
> and his glory will be seen upon you.
> And nations shall come to your light,
> and kings to the brightness of your rising. (Isa. 60. 1-3)

We also find the glory, being the symbol of Yahweh, connected with a cloud. This is, perhaps, a covering to hide the overwhelming power of God which would otherwise destroy all who saw it:

> These words the LORD spoke to all your assembly at the mountain out of the midst of the fire, the cloud, and the deep gloom, with a loud voice; . . . and you said, "Behold, the LORD our God has shown us his glory and greatness, and we

have heard his voice out of the midst of the fire; we have this day seen God speak with man and man still live . . ."

(Deut. 5. 22, 24)

We have already noticed the passage (Ex. 24. 16) in which the presence of Yahweh on Mount Sinai is described in terms of "glory". The glory also describes the presence in the Jerusalem Temple:

> . . . when the priests came out of the holy place, a cloud filled the house of the LORD, so that the priests could not stand to minister because of the cloud; for the glory of the LORD filled the house of the LORD. (1 Kings 8. 10, 11)

This aspect of "glory" is sometimes confused with the post-Old Testament concept of the *shekinah*. Strictly, the *shekinah* is the "presence" of Yahweh, and the word is used frequently in the Targums when it is wanted to say that God has a particular dwelling place, or is particularly revealed in a certain way (especially in the Temple), while at the same time safeguarding the omnipresence of God. It may be translated "the universal presence of Yahweh as it is revealed in a particular way or place". With the introduction of this doctrine, which is not found in the Old Testament itself, we get completely away from all ideas of a purely localized presence of God.

CHAPTER THREE

THE NATURE OF MAN

We have seen that for the men of the Old Testament, God was not a matter for philosophical speculation, but a personal God who made himself known to them. That is to say, such doctrines as creation and salvation have meaning only when they are related to the Hebrew understanding of the nature of man and his place in the world. This has been looked at briefly when we were discussing the creation stories. We must now probe more deeply, and shall do it under four main headings:

(*a*) Man and his Make-up.
(*b*) Man and Society.
(*c*) Man, Sin, and Suffering.
(*d*) Man and his Destiny.

MAN AND HIS MAKE-UP

We are used to thinking of man as "body and soul" or perhaps "body, soul, and spirit" (with very vague ideas about the difference between "soul" and "spirit"!). This terminology is so common in our hymns and religious language generally that it is difficult to appreciate that it has no Biblical roots, and that it is derived much more from Plato than from Moses! In general, Greek thought considered man as a spirit imprisoned in a body, from which it sought release: there was a real di- (or tri-)

chotomy. Such a separation is quite alien to any Hebrew idea. For him, man was a unity. It is perfectly true that we find in our Old Testament words which the English versions translate as "soul", "spirit", and so on, but we ought not to give these words their everyday significance. This comes out when we think of the word "body". *We* can use the word with two meanings—either the material part of a living creature, or a corpse after death; this is because we are thinking in Greek terms of a body inhabited or deserted by the spirit. The Hebrew thought quite differently. A living body was a person, an individual: a corpse was something quite different. There is, therefore, no Hebrew word which we can use in the same way that we use "body" and there is no possibility of using the expression "dead body"—that would have been a contradiction. Living man was a unity, and it is essential that we remember this when we think of the various expressions used to describe man and his functions. For, of course, different words were used for different activities, and as we think of them we shall appear to be carving man up into his different parts. We are only justified in doing so if we remember at the same time that we are quite unjustified!

The main words with which we shall be concerned are:

i. *nephesh* usually translated "soul" or "life".

ii. *basar* usually translated "flesh".

iii. *dam* and its plural *dammim* usually translated "blood".

iv. *leb* and *lebab* usually translated "heart".

v. *ruach* usually translated "spirit".

In addition, we shall have to notice briefly the way in which psychological functions are attributed to various parts of the body: the eyes, the mouth, the kidneys, etc.

i. *"Life-soul"*—nephesh

The root meaning is "breath", but it is difficult to find a single word which satisfactorily translates *nephesh* into English. "Soul", "life", "mind" are all common in the English versions, and each corresponds with one meaning of the word. But here are many places where other English words would get the meaning better. "Breathing creature" will not do at all. "Person" or "personality" have been suggested, but "personality" has a more specialized meaning, while animals too are referred to as *nephesh*. Perhaps the best way of putting it is that *nephesh* refers to the individual as a total being in all his aspects apart from the purely physical (although when we make this distinction we must remember our warning about the unity of man). If we must have a translation, perhaps the least unsatisfactory is "selfhood", or even on occasions "-self".

In Gen. 2, *nephesh* refers to the primal man:

> ... the LORD God formed man of dust from the ground, and breathed into his nostrils the breath of life; and man became a living being (*nephesh chayyah*). (Gen. 2. 7)

Notice that the Hebrew does not say, as we would, that man received life, or received soul: man *became nephesh*. Precisely the same expression is used in v. 19 of the animals:

> ... the LORD God formed every beast of the field and every bird of the air ... and whatever the man called every living creature (*nephesh chayyah*) that was its name.

So that in many cases *nephesh* simply means the individual himself:

> Let me die the death of the righteous,
>   and let my end (*lit*: the end of my *nephesh*) be like his!
> (Num. 23. 10)

The *nephesh* is the seat of the desires:

MAN AND HIS MAKE-UP

> ... a man to whom God gives wealth, possessions, and honour, so that he lacks nothing of all that he (*lit*: his *nephesh*) desires ... (Eccles. 6. 2)

and of the emotions and passions (even being applied to God!)—

revulsion :

> And I will make my abode among you, and my soul (*nephesh*) shall not abhor you. (Lev. 26. 11)

> Be warned, O Jerusalem,
>   lest I (*lit*: my *nephesh*) be alienated from you. (Jer. 6. 8)

grief :

> Did not I weep for him whose day was hard?
>   Was not my soul (*nephesh*) grieved for the poor?
>   (Job 30. 25)

and joy :

> I will greatly rejoice in the LORD,
>   my soul (*nephesh*) shall exult in my God. (Isa. 61. 10)

In all these cases we shall note that though we could think of *nephesh* as being part of the individual, the sense is just as good, or better, if we simply think of *nephesh* as the total individual in the act of feeling that emotion. The same applies to thinking and mental acts generally :

> ... Mordecai told them to return answer to Esther, "Think not (*lit*: think not in thy *nephesh*) that in the king's palace you will escape any more than all the other Jews ..."
>   (Esther 4. 13)

We need to be clear, therefore, that when we read "soul" or "mind" in the Old Testament, we must not give these words their usual English meaning. If we do we shall be led sadly astray.

ii. *"Flesh"*—basar

There are two ideas commonly associated with "flesh" that have no relation to Old Testament usage. The first is that flesh is contrasted with spirit in such a way as to imply inferiority. We have noted in Greek thought the suggestion that the spirit is imprisoned in the body; this can easily be seen to imply that if the spirit is good, that which imprisons it is opposed to it, and therefore evil. In the Old Testament there is certainly a contrast between flesh and spirit, but it is a contrast of strength and weakness (e.g. Isa. 31. 3) or of man and God (e.g. Ps. 56. 4). But "flesh" is specifically used for the attitude which walks in the ways of God (Ezek. 11. 19, 20), and there is never any suggestion of opposition between the two, nor even that they are different forms of existence (except where "spirit" is applied to God). In Ps. 16. 9, 10 flesh, spirit, heart, and glory are all found together, almost interchangeably:

> Therefore my heart is glad, and my soul (*lit*: glory) rejoices;
>   my body (*lit*: flesh) also dwells secure.
> For thou dost not give me (*lit*: my *nephesh*) up to Sheol,
>   or let thy godly one see the Pit.

The second is to read into Old Testament usage St Paul's way of using "flesh" to imply man's lower nature (e.g. Rom. 7. 14: "I am carnal, sold under sin ... I do not do what I want, but I do the very thing I hate"), so that flesh and spirit oppose one another as two natures in the one individual (cf. Gal. 5. 16-24). It is true that flesh may become corrupt or act corruptly (e.g. Gen. 6. 12), but then, so may *nephesh* (e.g. Mic. 6. 7). The fact is that *basar* is morally neutral. Like man himself, it is capable of either good or evil. We may define it as "the material manifestation of *nephesh*", and just as *nephesh* often means simply "the man himself", often enough *basar* could be translated the same way (e.g. Ps. 84. 2, where it is used with "heart" in parallel with *nephesh*).

There is, however, an extension to this meaning. Human relationship is, quite obviously, a matter of fleshly generation (cf. Gen. 2. 23), and unity of flesh means human relationship, whether natural (Gen. 37. 27) or marital (Gen. 2. 24). As we have noted, flesh is contrasted with God as being weak and subject, and it is clear that all humanity shares the same nature. *Basar* is therefore used with the significance of "humanity" or "mankind" (Gen. 6. 12, 13; Isa. 66. 23, etc.) or even "every living thing" (Gen. 9. 11-17).

Occasionally the meaning crops up of "the material substance composing the body", whether alive or dead (e.g. Ex. 12. 8, referring to the cooking of the flesh of the Paschal lamb), but it is best to allow this meaning only when it is clearly required by the context.

iii."*Blood*"—dam, *and its plural* dammim

The primary reference is, of course, to the physical substance of blood. This is, however, closely connected with both *basar* and *nephesh*. The text which gives us the main clue is Leviticus 17. 11, 14 :

> For the life (*nephesh*) of the flesh (*basar*) is in the blood.

and

> For the life of every creature is the blood of it (*lit*: For the *nephesh* of all *basar* is its blood in its *nephesh*).

The implication is that the *nephesh* finds its seat in the blood. It is not hard to see how this sort of thinking came about. As the blood ebbs from a wound in the body, so life becomes weaker, finally ceasing altogether. When death occurs, the effusion of blood ceases. Conversely, if a corpse is cut, no blood flows. The implication is obvious: the life is in the blood.[1]

So, blood which has been shed by violent means is considered to be still alive. Cain is told:

> The voice of your brother's blood is crying to me from the
> ground. (Gen. 4. 10)

In one way this understanding of the connection of life and blood would be academic, if it were not for the connection of blood and sacrifice. We shall have to consider this matter in more detail when we look at sacrificial thinking, but here we may note that though the essence of animal sacrifice is the slaughter of the victim, the object is not death, but the release of life, that is, the blood. That the victim has to die in order to free the blood for the sacrificial ritual is, strictly speaking, irrelevant.

iv. *"Heart"*—leb, lebab

Again, these two words are closely connected etymologically, and have almost exactly the same meaning. The use of "heart" is very close to that of *nephesh*: but whereas *nephesh* relates to the whole of a man's individuality, "heart" is concerned specifically with what we would call the psychical functions. It is connected closely with *nephesh* in a number of passages, e.g.,

> But from there you will seek the LORD your God, and you will
> find him, if you search after him with all your heart and with
> all your soul. (Deut. 4. 29)

In many cases, the right translation would be "mind" rather than "heart", and there is frequent reference to the

[1] Other passages seem to imply that life is connected with breath (e.g. Gen. 7. 22). The reason is very much the same as for blood. Had the question arisen about the relation between these two concepts, the answer, no doubt, would have been that the outward manifestation of the indwelling life was the act of breathing.

act of the will in living an upright life:

> O Lord, the God of Abraham, Isaac, and Israel, our fathers, keep for ever such purposes and thoughts in the hearts of thy people, and direct their hearts towards thee. Grant to Solomon my son that with a whole heart he may keep thy commandments, thy testimonies, and thy statutes . . .
> (1 Chron. 29. 18, 19)

and in sinning:

> Yet they sinned still more against him,
>   rebelling against the Most High in the desert.
> They tested God in their heart . . . (Ps. 78. 17, 18)

> When the king of Egypt was told that the people had fled, the mind (*lebab*) of Pharaoh and his servants was changed towards the people . . . (Ex. 14. 5)

The heart is the seat of conscience:

> I hold fast my righteousness, and will not let it go;
>   my heart does not reproach me for any of my days.
> (Job. 27. 6)

but also of pride:

> The man of haughty looks and arrogant heart . . . (Ps. 101. 5)

It is used occasionally, here being very close to *nephesh*, as needing physical sustenance, so that these psychical functions may be better fulfilled:

> . . . that he may bring forth food from the earth,
>   and wine to gladden the heart of man,
> oil to make his face shine,
>   and bread to strengthen man's heart. (Ps. 104. 14, 15)

It is also the seat of the emotions: sadness (1 Sam. 1. 8), miserliness (Deut. 15. 9, 10), fear (Deut. 28. 65), anger (Deut. 19. 6, where R.S.V. "in hot anger" is, literally, "when his heart is hot".), courage (Ps. 31. 24, and Dan.

11. 25, where R.S.V. translates *lebab* as "courage"). It is the seat of joy and gladness (Judges 18. 20; 1 Kings 8. 66) and is frequently associated with drunkenness (Ruth 3. 7; 2 Sam. 13. 28). Almost all the passions and emotions are predicated, somewhere or other, of the heart.

To sum up, we may say that to the Hebrew the heart was the seat of almost all the functions that we associate with our English words "mind", "will", "conscience", and "emotions". The brain did not come into it, and in fact the word never occurs in the Old Testament: the Hebrew seems to have had no idea at all of its place in human activity.

v. *"Spirit"*—ruach

Ruach has four main meanings. It is applied to the physical breath (Ps. 135. 17; Lam. 4. 20); to the wind (Gen. 8. 1; Ex. 15. 10); to the spirit of man; and to the Spirit of God. We shall consider the Spirit of God in the next chapter (pp. 128-32, below), and in this section we shall be thinking about its third meaning, the spirit of man.

In all its uses there is a feeling of transitoriness. The wind comes and goes; the breath of man is fleeting and its departure unpredictable; the Spirit of God is quite outside the control, and even the understanding, of man. In the same way, the *ruach* of man almost always has reference to temporary conditions or emotions. In this respect it differs from *nephesh* and *lebab,* both of which, on the whole, describe settled dispositions of character and personality. There is also the feeling of energy and power, ready to break out at any moment.

A good example of the connection of outward and inward meanings of *ruach* is seen in the way in which it is applied both to the heavy breathing typical of anger, and then also to anger itself, e.g. in Job 4. 9 R.S.V. "blast of his anger" is literally *"ruach* of his nostrils". In a similar

MAN AND HIS MAKE-UP

way *ruach* is connected with liveliness, activity, and animation, e.g. Judges 15. 19:

> ... when he drank, his spirit returned, and he revived.

Cf. 1 Sam. 30. 12. It comes in the opposite way in Ex. 6. 9:

> ... they did not listen to Moses, because of their broken spirit ...

Impatience is typical of *ruach*, as in Prov. 14. 29, where R.S.V. "he who has a hasty temper" is literally "the short in *ruach*". It is also connected with impulses, often under the direction of Yahweh (e.g. 2 Chron. 36. 22; Hag. 1. 14; Ezra 1. 5; Jer. 51. 11). In each case the implication is that those concerned were acting under overwhelming compulsion, in many cases in a way quite different from what would normally be expected.

It is in a similar way that we understand the prophetic spirit which some men exhibit from time to time (cf. 2 Kings 2. 15; Ezek. 13. 3), and especially prophetic "ecstasy" (see pp. 114-17, below). It also is the spirit of desire (Isa. 26. 9) and distress (1 Sam. 1. 15).

When these two ideas, the breath denoting life given by God, and the inspired spirit stirred up by God to action, come together, it is not surprising to find that *ruach* comes to denote something not dissimilar to what we know as "spirit", dwelling in *basar*, not natural, but God-given:

> Thus says God, the LORD ...
>   who gives breath (*neshamah*) to the people upon it
>   and spirit (*ruach*) to those who walk in it. (Isa. 42. 5)

> O God, the God of the spirits of all flesh ... (Num. 16. 22)

which passes away at death:

> My spirit (*ruach*) is broken, my days are extinct,
>   the grave is ready for me. (Job 17. 1)

In general, therefore, we may say that so far as man is concerned, *ruach* has two main meanings: the irrational, impulsive nature; and that part of man's nature which responds to the promptings of God. We may doubt whether the Hebrew would have made any clear distinction between them.

vi. *The psychical functions of bodily organs*

We must also notice other parts of the body which were thought of as having psychical functions. The kidneys (reins) are sometimes spoken of as the seat of right conduct or conscience, often in a way which is synonymous with some usages of "heart". There are, for instance, a number of passages (e.g. Jer. 11. 20; 12. 2; Ezek. 33. 31) in which R.S.V. actually translates *kelayoth,* "kidneys", as "heart". An instructive passage is Ps. 7. 9, where R.S.V. "minds and hearts" is literally "hearts and kidneys".

In a similar way, the eyes discriminate between good and evil (Hab. 1. 13), the mouth produces speech, not merely as a physical action, but as a responsible organ, the neck is connected with pride ("stiff neck"), and so on.

The men of Old Testament times did not have, as we do, knowledge of a unifying centre of consciousness and direction. They *did* have the experience that often enough things were said or judgements passed without real conscious effort at all. We attribute such experiences to "instinct": the Hebrew attributed them to the parts of the body which seemed to be concerned. Nevertheless, we must not run away with the idea that he thought of man as a jumble of bits slung together, each bit with its own function. Man was a unity, and all these were aspects of the one man, all were interdependent, and, most important, if man was to be what he ought to be, all were to be brought under the control of Yahweh.

Before we leave this subject, we ought to emphasize that

we cannot dogmatize about the precise meanings of these words. Hebrew has no carefully defined and scientifically selected vocabulary to express exact significance. Its meanings overlap, and what one man might call *ruach*, another might call *lebab*, and yet another *nephesh*; such marginal cases are bound to occur. We must remember also that the Old Testament literature was written over a period of several hundred years. Just as English usage has changed since the time of Chaucer, or even since the Authorized Version, so also over the centuries Hebrew use of words changed.

In looking at these terms, we may have been tempted to think of using the term "Hebrew psychology", as indeed some writers have done. This is a phrase which is best avoided, since to us the word "psychology" implies a disciplined, descriptive science, and the Hebrews certainly had nothing of the kind. We are here dealing with popular use of words, and trying to see as far as possible what they meant, so that we may interpret more clearly what the various writers are trying to say to us.

MAN AND SOCIETY

There are two main ways of considering man's relations with his fellows. We may either think of each separate individual first, and then of their coming together to form the larger units of family, clan, and nation, in which case we shall probably conclude that "society" exists for the sake of the individual; or we may think of "society" first, and the individual only as a member of the units to which he belongs, and we shall probably conclude that the individual exists for the sake of the whole. If we to-day were faced with this choice, we would almost certainly choose the former, and modern Western European thought is based on it. Many, indeed, would say, without having given the matter much thought, that this, and this only, could be the Biblical viewpoint. It is a good example of the way in which we tend to use the Bible to bolster up our own ideas rather than to look at it to see what it really says.

Realist as always, the Hebrew knew without any shadow of doubt that the life of man apart from the greater unit was impossible. In the harder conditions of life then, it was self-evident that man on his own would die, and die quickly. (It is not so evident, though just as true, in the conditions of life to-day.) Moreover, he knew that the life of each individual was closely affected by what his fellows did, and that what each did affected the whole of the society in which he lived. Man *could* not exist apart from the greater whole. The Old Testament, therefore, reverses the modern Western order, and in general puts "society" first.[2] It is this sense of the way in which things do, as a matter of experience, happen that accounts for a good deal of what seems to us unethical and immoral in the story of Israel.

The classic example, and the one always quoted, is that of Achan in Joshua 7. Before the attack on Jericho, Joshua had proclaimed that the entire city was to be "devoted", destroyed as an offering to Yahweh, as a sort of "firstfruits" of the Promised Land. No Israelite was to take any of the spoil of the city for himself (Josh. 6. 17-19). Achan, however, broke this *tabu*, and in effect stole from Yahweh. The result was the anger of Yahweh; but it fell, not just on Achan, but on the whole nation (7. 10ff). In order to rid themselves of the offender, and so turn away the wrath of Yahweh, the sacred lot is used. As a result, guilt is fastened, first on the tribe of Judah, then the clan of the Zerachites, then the house of Zabdi, and finally on the offender, Achan.

[2] Though we must beware of this word "society". The Hebrew never thought in such abstract terms: "family", yes; "clan", yes; "tribe", yes; "Israel", yes; but an abstract "society", no!

MAN AND SOCIETY

Achan confesses his sin, and in order to root out the blemish from the nation he is put to death, and the stolen goods destroyed with him. But not only Achan; with him are destroyed his family, his animals, and his possessions, everything to which his influence has extended.

Now, whatever we think of this story from the moral viewpoint of later Christianity, it is clearly most instructive in telling us about what the Israelites of the time thought about the relationship between the individual and the larger groups. What Achan did affected them all. We shall, too, almost certainly be wrong if we think of the rooting out of his family as a punishment: whatever Achan may have done, his family seems to have had nothing to do with the affair, and how could his animals be involved anyway? The point is, rather, that Achan must be rooted out of Israel, and since his family, flocks, and goods are affected by him, and are to some extent an extension of him, they must go also. It is a process of racial cleansing rather than anything else.

It is this which underlies the statement in Ex. 20. 5 that Yahweh visits the sins of the fathers upon the children, even to the third and fourth generation. Besides the obvious point that some kinds of sin really did affect the children physically (and, as we are only now starting to appreciate, psychologically), the children were, in fact, liable to suffer penalty, or even death, for the sins of the father. In the same way, the "blood feud" is well known in Israel (cf. 2 Sam. 3. 27-30; 14. 5-7); the curse on Gehazi is pronounced on his descendants also (2 Kings 5. 27); the Gibeonites insist that seven of the sons of Saul shall be put to death for the sin of Saul against them (2 Sam. 21. 1-9). Other instances could be quoted, particularly from the early period. This has been called both "the defective sense of individuality" and "corporate personality". "Corporate personality" seems to imply a loss of individual personality, which is far from being the case, and it is best to think of it as an interpenetration between the individual and the groups to which he belongs.

It is here that we must make a distinction that a Hebrew almost certainly would not have made, between individual religion and individual ethical and political responsibility. By individual religion we mean that sense of personal communion with the Divine which has been described as "the flight of the alone to the alone", or which led A. N. Whitehead to define religion as "what a man does with his solitariness". By individualism in ethics and politics we mean that we account each man responsible both in law and before God for his own actions, and those only, and think of each individual as having a value in his own right which must be respected. It is not difficult for us to make this separation, and to realize that either may exist without the other. For the Hebrew, at any rate down to the eighth century, religious, political, and ethical life were so unified that the distinction could not have even been perceived.

"Personal religion" in the Old Testament finds its high-water mark in the life of Jeremiah. This introspective man, desperately longing for human friendship and companionship, is cut off from it by his fixed determination to speak the Word of God, in season, out of season; as a consequence, he is thrown back on God, with whom he talks "as a man talks to a friend" (see, e.g., 20. 7ff; 12. 1ff, etc.). This deepening of personal communion with God was no doubt intensified by his being virtually cut off from worship in the Temple for some part, at least, of his life (36. 5). For most men, to be cut off from the cultus would have been to be cut off from Yahweh entirely (cf. 1 Sam. 26. 19): for Jeremiah it only deepened his personal communion with Yahweh, and it is true to say that here there is a new element in religion. But although it is new, the seeds of it are back in the past. Israel, as we have seen, is the covenant people, and their worship is the worship of a nation. Its focus is the cultus, whether carried out at Jerusalem, at the Northern shrines of Dan and Bethel, at Shiloh or Gilgal, or at one of the local sanctuaries. Religion *was* the sharing in the cultus. Even here, however, the individual did not merely act as a member of the nation. He could, and did, make individual family sacrifices (1 Sam. 1. 3, 21; 2. 13). Some men, at least, were conscious that Yahweh had a message and purpose for them as individuals, to which they had to make personal response (many examples could be taken, from Moses onwards). Quite clearly, the psalms are a treasure house of personal religion; and though detailed argument from them would be hazardous in the present state of scholarly opinion about the book, recent work, on the whole, links the psalms firmly with cultic worship, and puts many more of them in the pre-Exilic period than scholars of an earlier generation would have allowed. Without, therefore, wishing in any way to detract from the greatness of Jeremiah, who stands out as one of the great men of the Old Testament, it is fair to say that he taught as he did because of his Hebrew inheritance, rather than, as is sometimes implied, in spite of it.

When we look at the other element, individual responsibility in ethics and politics, we may contrast with the story of Achan the teaching of Ezekiel (18, and all through the book), that a man stands or falls by what he himself does. This teaching of Ezekiel is not original: it follows quite conclusively from all the teachings of the earlier prophets, even though not explicitly stated, and finds an expression in so many words in the Code of Deuteronomy itself (Deut. 24. 16). This, too, has its roots in the Exodus faith, even though not explicitly, for in the prophets it is based on their overwhelming sense of the justice and love of God, and this, as we have seen, is basic to Israel's understanding of the nature of their Covenant God.

We may sum all this up by saying that Israel never forgets its corporate nature. Even when individualism is most explicit, it is within the context of both the national worship and the national unity in action. Nevertheless, it is within the Exodus faith that individualism can grow and take its proper place in a world which starts off with a "defective sense of individuality", and it is from this Hebrew tradition that our Western ideas have developed.

DETACHED NOTE:
"ISRAEL" AND THE RACIAL UNITY OF THE HEBREWS

The fact is that there is no real racial unity of Israel. They derive their unity as a nation from their common acceptance of the covenant faith rather than from any ties of blood. It is later tradition that they were the descendants of Abraham, and no doubt a nucleus of Hebrews could legitimately claim that descent. But round them had gathered many other groups. The invasions of Joshua led to a period of inter-racialism in which Canaanite and Hebrew grew together until the distinction was lost (cf. Judges 1. 21ff). Kenites were found in Israel (Judges 1. 16; 4. 11), and the Calebites seem originally to have been separate, perhaps connected with Edom. Inter-marriage brought alien blood into Israel (e.g. Judges 14. 1ff; 2 Sam. 11. 3ff), even into the royal house itself (e.g. 1 Kings 11. 1ff). No doubt this was intensified by the importation of alien mercenaries for the army (e.g. 2 Sam. 15. 18). See also Deut. 26. 5; Ezek. 16. 3.

The relationship of the ancestry of Israel to the various tribes, and the question whether tribal relationships can be taken as an indication of differing ancestry, is extremely difficult, and no certain answer can be given. What is quite clear is that to call the Jews "Semites" is to beg every possible question. What holds Israel together is not common blood but common membership in the covenant. It is true that with the growth of national unity traditions develop so as to suggest a unity of origin, and this tends to strengthen the unity of Israel. But, nevertheless, Israel is, and always has been, a concept based on religious grounds rather than race, and hence it has been in the past a missionary religion and will still accept converts to-day, although not engaging in overt missionary activity.

We may also mention the connection of religion and land. That there was a feeling that Israel's God could only be worshipped on Israelite soil is shown by such passages as 1 Sam. 26. 19 and 2 Kings 5. 17. Ps. 42. 3ff describes the exile from Judaea longing to come once more to worship Yahweh on his holy hill. But the very fact that Canaan was not Israel's native land, but a country won by conquest *after* they had become the covenant people, makes it impossible for them ever to consider that God could *only* be worshipped on Palestinian soil. Such ideas may have been popularly held, but the Exile makes it quite clear that they are false. It is this which has made possible the survival of Judaism when other religions of the ancient world are dead and forgotten. It has gone hand in hand with monotheistic faith to maintain and expand the worship of Yahweh wherever the Covenant people have gone, even though alongside it has gone a very real sense of the importance of Jerusalem, which has to be recognized to-day in the sphere of international politics.

MAN, SIN, AND SUFFERING

"Sin" is one of those words everyone thinks he understands, but which turn out on examination to be by no means as clear as appears on the surface. Once more, it will be necessary to examine the words used. There are a considerable number, but they are conveniently grouped into four classes, and only the main words in each group need be discussed. They are:

i. A deviation from the right way. The main word is *chatta'th*: similar meanings are found in *'awon* (iniquity) and *shagah* (to err).

ii. A changed status, of guilt as opposed to innocence. It is much more a legal concept than moral, though there is a closer connection than might appear on the surface. Main words are *'asham* and *rasha'*.

iii. Rebellion against a superior, closely connected with the breaking of a covenant. The main word here is *pesha'*.

iv. A group of words which describe sin. It is folly, vanity, or uselessness, or bad in the general sense of the word, that is, offensive, unpleasant, disagreeable. The words *ra'* and *ra'ah* have a very wide connotation, just like the English word "bad", and are very widely used.

It will not be necessary to go into the usage of this final group. They are descriptions of the effect of sin and the attitude of men towards it, rather than being concerned with the nature of sin itself. The other groups will call for closer attention.

Perhaps the most important group is the third, sin as rebellion. We have seen how the whole religious life of the nation is founded on the Covenant: to go against the declared will of God is rebellion, *pesha'*. It is frequently translated in our English versions as "transgress" or "trespass", but this is wholly inadequate. The corresponding verb is used in the secular sense meaning "to rebel" in 1 Kings 12. 19; 2 Kings 1. 1; 3. 5, 7, of subject nations rising against their overlords. It may also be used of a rebellion by an individual against his superior, e.g. by Jacob against Laban:

What is my offence (*pesha'*)? What is my sin (*chatta'th*), that
you have hotly pursued me?   (Gen. 31. 36)

In Ex. 22. 9, the words translated by R.S.V. as "breach of
trust" (in this case, breach of a commercial agreement) are,
literally, "word of rebellion" (*debar pesha'*). It may also be
used of rebellion by subject against king, as in 1 Sam. 24. 11
where R.S.V. translates *pesha'* as "treason".

This idea of rebellion is found in the religious sense,
particularly of man's revolt against God:

Sons have I reared and brought up,
  but they have rebelled against me.   (Isa. 1. 2)

that is, they have been living apart from the Covenant. For
Isaiah and the other prophets, of course, this rebellion is
not so much a neglect of religious duties—the nation is only
too willing to perform these—but neglect of their duties to
their neighbours, as even a casual reading of the rest of the
chapter will show. A similar idea may be found in
Amos 5. 12.

Pesha' is a stronger word than *chatta'th*, to which we
will turn in a moment. This is shown, for example in Job
34. 36, 37:

Would that Job were tried to the end,
  because he answers like wicked men.
For he adds rebellion (*pesha'*) to his sin (*chatta'th*);
  . . . and multiplies his words against God.

Even so, the wicked man may return from his rebellion into
the favour of God:

Because he considered and turned away from all the transgressions (*pesha'*) which he had committed, he shall surely
live. . . .   (Ezek. 18. 28)

This, however, is only by the mercies of God. There is no
provision made in any of the legal codes for sacrifice in

respect of deliberate sin committed "with a high hand", and in P such sin is expressly excluded (Num. 15. 28-31). The only cure for rebellion is a penitential return to the one whose covenant has been broken, trusting in his mercy.

Chatta'th is the most important word of the first group, sin as a deviation from the right way. Again, the secular use of the corresponding verb *chata'* helps us to see the meaning. It is used in Judges 20. 16 :

> . . . seven hundred picked men who were left-handed; every one could sling a stone at a hair, and not miss (*chata'*).

where it simply means to miss a target. It is used of missing one's way, and hence following a wrong path :

> It is not good for a man to be without knowledge,
> and he who makes haste with his feet misses (*chata'*) his way (Prov. 19. 2)

or of lacking something that ought to be present :

> You shall know that your tent is safe,
> and you shall inspect your fold and miss nothing. (Job 5. 24)

that is, nothing that ought to be there is missing. Hence, it becomes used of missing the way of right or duty, either against another man :

> Then Saul said, "I have done wrong (*chata'*); return, my son David, for I will no more do you harm . . ." (1 Sam. 26. 21)

or, more usually, against God, as when Jonathan has broken the *tabu* against food in 1 Sam. 14. 38 :

> Come hither, all you leaders of the people; and know and see how this sin (*chatta'th*) has arisen to-day . . .

As here, much of its usage is of unintentional sin. But it is also used of deliberate sin, arising from temptation which

MAN, SIN, AND SUFFERING

ought to be conquered but is not (cf. Gen. 4. 7). The fact that the word can be used in both senses reminds us of the frailty of man, the ease with which he falls into wrong ways, and of the love of God which will take him back.

These two groups of words have described the nature of sin. The final group is concerned not so much with the sin itself, but with the changed status of the sinner. He is guilty, no longer innocent. *Rasha‘* is used, for instance, in Num. 35. 31:

> ... you shall accept no ransom for the life of a murderer who is guilty (*rasha‘*) of death; but he shall be put to death.

"Guilty of death" means that he is guilty (of murder) and so in such a wrong relationship with the community that his death is the only solution. This concept of guilt is obviously much more legalistic, a fact that is emphasized by the fact that it needs to be a verdict pronounced by a court. As we have seen, there is plenty of evidence to show that there was frequent injustice done in the courts, and that often enough the guilty could be pronounced innocent if the bribe was large enough. We need, then, to remember that Yahweh also is involved: even though a human court pronounces innocence, God is still God, and will by no means clear the guilty. There is a changed status, not only before men, but before Yahweh, and this cannot be altered by any human decree. It can only be restored by the free action of the guilty man, who confesses his sin, makes restitution as far as is possible, and offers the appropriate sacrifice. The sacrifices provided are known by the same names as are used for sin, *chatta'th* (sin offering) and *‘asham* (guilt offering). The regulations are found in Lev. 4. 1— 6. 7. Both types of sacrifice are post-exilic, and the exact difference between them is difficult for us to determine, though it seems probable that the *‘asham* is particularly concerned with offences where restoration is possible (Lev.

5. 16), and the *chatta'th* where no such material restitution can be made.[3]

If we look through these chapters, we shall notice some interesting points. The sin concerned is always to some extent involuntary. The one case mentioned where there can be no doubt that it is deliberate (withholding evidence when called on to give it, 5. 1) it is expressly stated "he shall bear his iniquity". It may be that the sin was committed in blameworthy circumstances (e.g. 5. 4, rash oaths), but this is a different story. The Old Testament knows the frailty of man, and knows that these things do happen, and must be provided for. But *deliberate* sin is an act of the will, coming from the character of the man, and he must accept the consequences.

We also notice that the offences listed are very mixed: they range from the sin of a ruler in departing from the law of Yahweh (4. 22) to the unwitting incurring of ceremonial uncleanness by touching the carcase of an unclean creature (5. 2). This apparent equation of ritual offences with moral faults strikes us as strange and lacking in ethical sense. But in fact the Hebrew was far from making this equation. It is true that the ritual prescribed in each case is the same, but that is because the purpose is the same. When a man committed a moral offence, he cut himself off from Yahweh by breaking the terms of the covenant: if he committed a ritual offence, he was cut off from joining in the worship of the nation. In each case, the purpose of the sacrifice was to make a ceremonial re-entry into full participation in the cultus, which in the case of moral offences could only be after repentance, an element not required for ritual faults.

Finally, we see that guilt is not affected by ignorance of

[3] But we notice that the 'asham is also used for the removal of ceremonial defilement (Lev. 5. 2-6). The interpretation of ritual texts is always difficult in the absence of a living liturgical tradition.

MAN, SIN, AND SUFFERING 99

the law in question, or even by ignorance that an offence has in fact been committed. Morally, of course, we cannot condemn a man in such circumstances; but nevertheless the law has been broken, the regular order of things has been changed, and restoration must be effected.

With these points in mind, we may look at a few general ideas which are found in the Old Testament. These are not exhaustive, and a good deal more could be written. But they will suffice to give the basis for a deeper study of the subject, for which examination of words and their use by means of a work such as Young's *Analytical Concordance* is likely to be most profitable.

First, then, sin is not just something done, external to the individual. It goes much deeper: it affects the status of the man, by cutting him off from the Covenant; it affects his character, since the habit of sin, once acquired, is very difficult to eradicate; and it leads to retribution. This could be either from outside (e.g. from the person wronged), from the inevitable consequences of the act itself (as in contracting leprosy after entering affected premises),[4] or from Yahweh himself. Often enough Yahweh's punishment is seen as direct, as in the story of Gehazi in 2 Kings 5. 19-27,[5] although it is often seen in indirect ways (cf. Ps. 73. 18-20), and of course the exclusion from the cultus caused by sin was itself a real punishment. Particularly so is this the case where grievous sin leads to expulsion of the offender, where he is driven out from his people to fend for himself as best he may. Such a sinner might well echo

[4] Lev. 14. 33-47 provides that anyone who enters premises suspected of harbouring leprosy shall incur ceremonial defilement, and ritual washings have to be carried out. No doubt if an offender contracted leprosy it would be seen as punishment for breaking the law—rightly enough.

[5] Though in all probability we should see Gehazi's contraction of leprosy as the consequences of his using infected clothing!

the words of Cain (Gen. 4. 12-14), for he would indeed become an outlaw (as in the case of David, I Sam. 26. 19, 20).

Secondly, we have already noticed the way in which actions were thought of as affecting not only the doer, but also all those connected with him in family, clan, tribe, and nation. It is commonplace that this was believed to extend to sin also and this finds expression in the Ten Words (Ex. 20. 5) and many other places (cf. pp. 87ff, above). Hence the institution in post-exilic times of the rite of the Day of Atonement (Lev. 16), a solemn yearly sacrifice for the sins of the nation, not only corporate sins as such, but all which might affect the people as a whole—that is, all sin which had not been adequately atoned for during the year, either because of ignorance that sin had been committed, or because of inability to perform the rites for any reason.

Thirdly, we notice that in earlier times, and indeed right through the Old Testament, there is an emphasis on action rather than thought as the basis of sin. That action was right which was in accordance with "what ought to be done" (see, e.g., 2 Sam. 13. 12, "Such a thing is not done in Israel", Gen. 34. 7; Judges 19. 30; and other passages). The standard is "custom", and this has the force of law. Inevitably, custom is concerned with action, for actions are patent to all, but who knows the thoughts of the heart? It is true that under the influence of the prophets custom as the touchstone is, or tends to be, replaced by conformity to the nature of Yahweh; even so, acts tend to be judged by external appearance. That some, at least, held this line of thought in New Testament times is shown by our Lord's comments on some Pharisees, notably in Matt. 23, while the spiritualizing of morality is seen more in the Sermon on the Mount than anywhere in the Old Testament. Nevertheless, there are passages, notably in Psalms (e.g. Ps. 51. 6-12) where sin and purity are seen as inward, and not merely concerned with actions. It must also be remembered that we can never draw a distinct line between the thoughts of the heart and the acts of the body: thought expresses itself in action, and what a man is can usually be recognized by what he does. Even in cases of sheer hypocrisy, it is rare for the situation not to be recognized. This links, again, with what we have already seen about the unity of human nature (see pp. 76f, above). Nevertheless, this is one real weakness in Hebrew teaching about sin.

Fourthly, we must note the connection between sin and suffering. This takes up the theme above, that sin brings retribution. The "logical" argument might be stated thus: sin is a breach of "what ought to be", so also is suffering; therefore suffering is caused by sin. The "deduction" might be borne out by observing that in fact sin was extremely frequently followed by suffering (judicial punishment, revenge, or natural consequences). When men realize that Yahweh, too, is concerned with morality, it is only a short step to suggest that suffering for which no cause is apparent is to be explained by saying that only Yahweh knew of some secret sin, and that he was sending punishment. The problems that this raised did not become prominent until the time of the Exile; in a situation where men are convinced of the "solidarity" of society it is not difficult to believe that suffering is indeed the result of sin, even though the sin might be not one's own, but that of kinsfolk, forefathers, or indeed any member of the nation. The implication is not that in order to avoid suffering the individual had better find out where he had sinned and put it right, but that every member of the Covenant people must maintain custom and *Torah,* and so obviate such happenings as far as possible. With the rise of the more individualistic outlook in the sixth century, individual suffering came to be regarded as the result of individual sin: righteousness led to prosperity, and wrong-doing to retribution, even though it might not be immediate (Ps. 1; Ps. 37, especially verses 22 and 25; Ps. 73. 12-20). It is almost the theme of Proverbs, with its continual suggestion that righteousness is good because it leads to prosperity, and evil bad because it leads to destruction. In many ways this is valuable teaching, even if it is not the whole truth: often enough evil ways lead to retribution, and honesty usually is the best policy. But two real difficulties arise: "Why do the wicked flourish?" and, "Why do the righteous suffer?" Ps. 73 seeks to answer the first question by saying that the day of vengeance will surely come; but everyone must have known cases where it did not come, and where the evil man lived out his days in peace and prosperity. The second question is the theme of Job, the saga of a righteous man whom we know to be suffering undeservedly. The "comforters" all through propound the "orthodox" view that Job's trials must be caused by sin, and urge him to repent (4. 7-11; 8. 3-7; 11. 13-20, etc.). Job, conscious of his rectitude, refuses their advice— how *can* he take it? (See 6. 28-30 etc., and chapter 31, in which he expressly asserts his innocence and demands that if he *is* guilty his suffering shall continue.) It cannot be said that the solution propounded by the author of Job—that suffering is part of the providence of God, and cannot be questioned by man—is satisfactory either. The fact is that the problem of suffering is one which has no solution where there is no understanding of life beyond the grave, and even then difficult problems remain. However, we need to remember that, as we saw before, man is neither merely an individual nor merely a member of society. Often the suffering of one individual is caused by the sin or fault of another, just as it is often the result of his own shortcomings. At times, too, it is impossible for us to see the cause: it seems senseless, and we have to remember that in God's providence the apparently evil may turn out for good. But when all is said and done, the Hebrew was grappling with a problem which every nation and creed has always had to face, and many of his insights have real relevance to the situation, even though he was unable to make from them a complete picture.

DETACHED NOTE:
THE DOCTRINE OF ORIGINAL SIN

This is not an easy matter to discuss, since so many versions of the doctrine have been, and are, held and taught. If however, we look at what the Old Testament teaches and does not teach, we shall have some grounds for judging the validity of doctrines when they are presented to us.

In the first place, the Old Testament accepts without reserve the *fact* of the universality of sin. This is not a dogmatic statement, but a matter of empirical experience: "All men do sin". Such statements are found, for instance, in 1 Kings 8. 46; Ps. 143. 2; Prov. 20. 9; Eccles. 7. 20, and many other places. Men do sin, whether through neglect or ignorance, failure or wilful disobedience. Each individual must recognize this fact (and hence his own sinfulness), and do something about it.[6] Hebrew religion is not a perfectionist religion which has no time except for the "unco' guid", but a way of life which takes human nature as it is. Being realist, it accepts that all men do sin; but it also accepts that man is intended to be righteous and live in accordance with the Covenant of Yahweh. Therefore, where men do sin, it provides the means for restoration.

How then does sin originate? Philosophically minded theologians have given many answers, one of the most prevalent being the suggestion that the sin of Adam has been transmitted to all men through natural generation, so

[6] We may note that the story of Job is not an assertion that a fully righteous man *did* exist, but a drama which assumes that it was possible that a man might live and experience such things.

that sin is inborn in all. Variations on this theme have often suggested sin to be connected with the sexual instincts and urges. This is far from the Old Testament. The Hebrew, practical as always, accepted the fact of sin and did something about it; the question of its origin hardly concerned him. Often enough, passages are quoted from the Old Testament which seem to imply some such doctrines (e.g. Ps. 51. 5; 58. 3; or Isa. 48. 8). If we come to these passages with ideas of inborn sin in our minds, we shall find them in the texts. But if we try to see the general tenor of Old Testament thought, and to interpret such passages in accordance with it, we shall conclude that they are simply stating in the strongest possible terms that all men are indeed sinful right through their lives, hardly going further than Isaiah, "Woe is me! For I am lost; for I am a man of unclean lips, and I dwell in the midst of a people of unclean lips . . . " (Isa. 6. 5).

Two passages in particular, however, call for further examination: the story of the Garden of Eden in Genesis 2 and 3, and the note prefaced to the flood narrative (Gen. 6. 1-7).

In the Garden of Eden story, we hear how God created man first, then the rest of the animals, and finally woman. They were placed in a Garden where none of the difficulties of life was present; the only requirement was that they should abstain from the fruit of the tree of the knowledge of good and evil. Under temptation from the serpent, the man and the woman ate of the fruit, and were cast out of the garden and cursed with the trials of life. The story is familiar, but certain points need to be noted.

(*a*) There is no suggestion that through his act man has become sinful, in the sense of gaining a bias towards sin that will be passed on to his posterity. What man has gained is a knowledge of "good and evil". In all probability this phrase is simply another way of saying "all things" (cf.

THE DOCTRINE OF ORIGINAL SIN

"far and near"), and the clear implication is that by eating man has attained half the attributes of Godhead (cf. 3. 5, 22). Whether this be so or not, it is quite clear that "good and evil" cannot mean "sinful bias".

(b) The punishment is that man shall work for his living with toil and sweat, and that woman should fulfil her function of childbirth in pain and difficulty. It cannot be argued that being cast out from the garden implies banishment from the presence of God, as is sometimes done, since in the very next narrative God is seen active with men outside Eden.

(c) Nor can it be said that man is punished with mortality. Gen. 3. 22 is quite clear that man never had immortality, nor was he intended to have it; he is cast out of the garden lest he attempt to seize the eternal life to which he had no natural right. On the contrary, God gives man what he has no right to expect—a reprieve. The threat is that on the day that he eats the fruit he will die, but this is not carried out. We see here the mercy of God at work rather than his wrath.

Remembering these points as we read the narrative, we see that there is here no suggestion of a description of sin's origin, Rather, it is what is known technically as an "aetiological myth", that is, a story told to explain otherwise incomprehensible aspects of man's life, in this case the pain and sorrow of childbirth (as opposed to the almost effortless parturition of wild mammals), and the way in which the earth produces weeds rather than fruit unless it is laboriously cultivated. The essence of the sin is not in the fruit eaten, but in the disobedience to the command of Yahweh. We could paraphase the myth by saying that as soon as man becomes aware that some things are forbidden, he is tempted to do them, and so commit sin (cf. Rom. 7. 7ff). The myth, then, refers not so much to the origin of man's troubles as to the spiritual experience of everyman.

But this is very different from saying that we have an account of the origin of sin. The beginnings of that line of interpretation of the story are to be found not in the Old Testament but in the inter-Testamental period (see, e.g., Wisd. 2. 23, 24; Ecclus. 25. 24, though the meaning of the latter passage is by no means as clear as appears on the surface.)

The second passage, Gen. 6. 1-7, is extremely complicated, both linguistically and textually. In its present form it stands as a preliminary to the Flood narrative, explaining how "the wickedness of man was great in the earth" because humanity had become corrupted by inter-marriage with the "sons of God". But if we take, as we surely must, verses 1 to 4 as an isolated fragment, there is nothing in it at all to suggest that here is an explanation of the origin of sin. It may well have something in common with the Eden story, in trying to explain how man can exhibit so much in common with the Divine and yet remain mortal (we remember similar Greek stories). It is also clearly connected with the folk-lore story of the giants (*nephilim*), also mentioned in Num. 13. 33, though since we have only isolated references to the legend it is difficult to know its original form. In any case, 6. 1-4 cannot be thought of as a story involving anything like a doctrine of Original Sin. This being accepted, verses 5-7 fall into place as an example of what we have already mentioned, that humanity was utterly sinful in fact. That no doctrine even of the complete universality of sin is implied is shown by the way in which Noah is described as "a righteous man, blameless . . ." (6. 9).

There is one sentence in these verses that must be mentioned: "every imagination of the thoughts of his heart was only evil continually". The word for "imagination" is *yetzer*. It is used in a few places in the Old Testament (e.g. Deut. 31. 21; Isa. 26. 3), and seems to mean "inward disposition". In later times the Rabbis advanced the doctrines of the *yetzer hara'*, the "evil inclination" which is part of man's natural make-up and which leads him into sin. In some Rabbinic writings it is balanced by the *yetzer hattob*, the "good inclination", with the two seen as striving together for mastery over the individual. This teaching, however, does not imply a doctrine of Original Sin in the Adamic sense, but simply insists on the obvious fact that man *is* prone to sin. As such, it is probably as far as any Hebrew teaching on the subject can go.

THE DESTINY OF MAN

The Hebrews were as well aware as any nation of the reality of sin and the depth of degradation to which it could drag man. But this did not lead to pessimism. Alongside it went their firm conviction of the essential *dignity* of man (see pp. 62f, above). In spite of everything, his constant acts of revolt, the pitiful attempts to do right which so often went wrong, the disposition which seemed so often to drive him into sin, man was still the crown of God's creation, with a special place in his providence. He was to have dominion over all that God has made (Ps. 8. 6-8). It is this which explains how the nation developed that understanding which has been called "the Hebrew genius for religion". We might imagine that to overlay the sense of sin with the belief in the high place of man would be to encourage the over-optimistic attitude of "He's a good fellow, and 'twill all be well", but this is not so. The conjunction of the two beliefs leads rather to deep understanding both of what God wants from man, and how far man is from fulfilling it, and so leads him to accept the need to reform his ways and follow God. Judaism has often been accused of being a "religion of works" rather than of faith, and to some extent this is true. It accepts the fact that man can do what is right under the guidance of *Torah*, and this leads to man striving to know the will of God, and to put it into practice.[7]

We must never forget that "otherworldliness" has no part in Old Testament thinking. The ideal of man is that he should take his proper place in this world, obedient to God, and acting as his steward in bringing about the ideal of a God-centred world. In this purpose, Israel has a large part, since it is through Israel that all men are to come to know God, and Israel is to be, as it were, the leaven in the world. Individual men are to respond to the righteousness and holiness of God by becoming righteous and holy themselves, doing so as part of an Israel which accepts Yahweh's sovereignty. But this is entirely in this world; man is a creature, living in the material creation, and is totally different from the High God whose habitation is eternity. For the greater part of the Old Testament period there was, as we shall see, little idea of any meaningful life after death. Man's purpose and place was in this world only. It is true that the doctrine of life after death does start to develop right at the end of the Old Testament period, and this is developed in the Rabbinic and Pharisaic tradition. We notice, however, that even in New Testament times some Jews at least would deny the resurrection (Luke 20. 27, Acts 23, 8). After the Fall of Jerusalem, however, the sect concerned, the Sadducees, disappears from history, and from that time onwards orthodox Judaism has held firmly to belief in life after death.

If there is no belief in a future life, there can be no teachings parallel to those of Christianity that man is an inhabitant of two worlds, the material and temporal, and the

---

[7] It must also be remembered that belief in inherent depravity and sinfulness may well lead, not to penitence and return, but to despair. Hope, in these circumstances, can only be found in a doctrine of personal salvation such as is found in Christianity, but is not part of Old Testament religion.

eternal, of which the eternal is by far the more important (cf. St John's use of the phrase "eternal life"). St Paul, brought up in the Pharisaic tradition and convinced of the resurrection, can say, "If in this life only we have hope in Christ, we are of all men most miserable" (1 Cor. 15. 19, A.V.), but this would not be true of Old Testament thought in general. On the contrary, the Hebrew would say, with justification, "If in this life only we have hope in God, we are of all men most to be envied". To know God and to do his will was the supreme end of man: it was a reward in itself, and the means by which he would reap a material reward in this life.

LIFE AFTER DEATH

We have mentioned this briefly already. While there is, as we have said, little idea of a meaningful life after death, there is also no idea of death as total extinction. Rather, we find that the dead continue to live in the Underworld, *She'ol,* a region of emptiness, dreariness, silence, weakness, and forgetting:

> If I look for Sheol as my house,
>   if I spread my couch in darkness . . .   (Job 17. 13)

> . . . but the dead know nothing, and they have no more reward . . . their love and their hate and their envy have already perished, and they have no more for ever any share in all that is done under the sun.   (Eccles. 9. 5, 6)

and, lest we should think that this is simply the Preacher's peculiar outlook:

> Thou prevailest for ever against him, and he passes;
>   thou changest his countenance, and sendest him away.
> His sons come to honour, and he does not know it;
>   they are brought low, and he perceives it not.
> He feels only the pain of his own body,
>   and he mourns only for himself.   (Job 14. 20-2)

In *she'ol,* all are equal, the mighty with the insignificant, in an equality of weakness:

> The LORD has broken the staff of the wicked,
>   the sceptre of rulers . . .
> Sheol beneath is stirred up
>   to meet you when you come,
> it rouses the shades to greet you,
>   all who were leaders of the earth;
> it raises from their thrones
>   all who were kings of the nations.
> All of them will speak
>   and say to you:
> "You too have become weak as we!
>   You have become like us!"
> Your pomp is brought down to Sheol . . .
> maggots are the bed beneath you,
>   and worms are your covering.   (Isa. 14. 5, 9-11)

By far the worst aspect of *she'ol* is that it is cut off from Yahweh:

> For in death there is no remembrance of thee;
>   in Sheol who can give thee praise?   (Ps. 6. 5)

> For Sheol cannot thank thee,
>   death cannot praise thee;
> those who go down to the pit cannot hope
>   for thy faithfulness.   (Isa. 38. 18)

though later on this becomes softened, as in Ps. 139. 7, 8:

> Whither shall I go from thy Spirit?
>   Or whither shall I flee from thy presence?
> If I ascend to heaven, thou art there!
>   If I make my bed in Sheol, thou art there!

We notice that it was held to be possible for spirits to be brought up from *she'ol* by magic arts, as in the story of Saul and the witch of Endor (1 Sam. 28. 7-19), though this is certainly regarded as illegitimate (v. 9; cf. also Deut. 18.

11; Isa. 8. 19). This is not, of course, a doctrine of possible release from *she'ol*. There are very occasional hints that this may be possible (1 Sam. 2. 6; Ps. 49. 14, 15; Ps. 73. 24; Hos. 13. 14), though nothing is said of the way in which this could happen.

There are two passages in the Old Testament which imply clearly a bodily resurrection, both from the very latest strata :

> Thy dead shall live, their bodies shall rise.
>   O dwellers in the dust, awake and sing for joy!
> For thy dew is a dew of light,
>   and on the land of the shades thou wilt let it fall.
> (Isa. 26. 19)

> And many of those who sleep in the dust of the earth shall awake, some to everlasting life, and some to shame and everlasting contempt. (Dan. 12. 2)

In neither case is there any elaboration, and we are left to consider for ourselves what manner of resurrection the writers have in mind. It is important, however, for the study of later Jewish and of Christian doctrine, to remember that any Old Testament teaching about significant survival *must* inevitably involve some concept of bodily resurrection. This follows from what we saw earlier, that man is a unity and not a union of separate parts which could, theoretically, exist in isolation. The Hebrew could not conceive of any existence except a bodily existence, and hence comes both the insignificance of life in *she'ol,* and the resurrection as the means by which release from *she'ol* will come.

It is this lack of a definite doctrine of life after death which accounts for the way children were considered essentials for a full existence, and lack of posterity a great evil. A man lives on in his children and his children's children, who keep his name alive :

> For as the new heaven and the new earth
> which I will make
> shall remain before me, says the LORD;
> so shall your descendants and your name remain.
>
> (Isa. 66. 22)

whereas the wicked will be destroyed in their descendants:

> May his posterity be cut off;
> may his name be blotted out in the second generation!
> (Ps. 109. 13)

> I have seen this people, and behold, it is a stubborn people; let me alone, that I may destroy them and blot out their name from under heaven . . . (Deut. 9. 13, 14)

So important is it that a man should have posterity that in the event of a man dying without a son, his brother is to marry his wife, the first-born son of that union being reckoned as the child of the dead brother (Deut. 25. 5-10); it is explicitly stated that the purpose is "to perpetuate his brother's name in Israel". (There was also, of course, the aim of keeping the family land intact and in the family, cf. 1 Kings 21. 3). This theme is used to good effect in the story of Ruth (Ruth 4. 1-13). The mere fact, however, of the existence of an heir being so important is witness to the paucity of other doctrines of life after death.

CHAPTER FOUR

THE RELATIONS BETWEEN GOD AND MAN

The essence of the Covenant faith is a real communication between God and Israel, by which God makes his will known, and man responds in obedience, gratitude, and worship, In this chapter we shall examine under five main heads the ways in which this communication took place: prophecy and the prophets; *Torah*; personal religion; the work of the Spirit of God; cultus, sacrifice, and priesthood.

PROPHECY AND THE PROPHETS

"Prophecy" and "prophet" are words which had different meanings at different times. This is emphasized by an editorial comment in 1 Sam. 9. 9:

> Formerly in Israel, when a man went to enquire of God, he said, "Come, let us go to the seer"; for he who is now called a prophet was formerly called a seer.

The word used for seer is *ro'eh*, "one who sees". The nearest equivalent in English is "one who has second sight", and such people have been held in honour in all unsophisticated communities. Amos is referred to, mockingly, as a "seer" (Amos 7. 12), and the word is used in parallel with "diviners" in Mic. 3. 7. Since Samuel is referred to as a "seer", it appears that whereas in early days the office of seer was one of honour, in later times it fell into disrepute, and the term "prophet" was used instead—a strange inversion of usage as we shall see. Samuel, the seer, is credited with very diverse functions: he is not only king-maker and judge, he is also expected to be able to give directions for finding lost property (1 Sam. 9. 1ff)! Dreams and clairvoyance were certainly considered to be means by which the will of God could be known, particularly dreams (cf. Gen. chs. 40 and 41; Dan. 4, etc.), while in Joel 2. 28 the dreaming of dreams and seeing of visions are linked with prophecy as manifestations of the Spirit of God.

Much more important, however, was the prophet (*nabi'*). To us this word at once suggests the great prophets responsible for the books bearing their names, but these came only at the end of a long development. In the time of Samuel, prophets were indeed known, but some of the references show them to be quite different from our normal concept of a prophet. In 1 Sam. 10 we have the story of Saul and the band of prophets. They are going along in a group, playing musical instruments, when they are joined by Saul, upon whom comes the Spirit of God so that he was "turned into another man". The picture is filled out in 19. 18-24, where we find prophesying includes lying naked, presumably in some sort of trance. We may well connect with this the coming of the spirit on Saul in 1 Sam. 18. 10, when he "raved" (R.V. "prophesied"), and attempted to murder David. The picture given of prophecy is of a state in which the prophet is quite beside himself, apparently under the influence of an exterior compulsion which makes him act and speak in a way quite different from normal. This fits well with the picture of the prophets of Ba'al in 1 Kings 18. 20-9, shouting and raving, cutting themselves with swords and lances "after their custom". There is small wonder that the editor of 1 Samuel wanted to make it quite clear that there was no connection between these men and the great prophets who were known and venerated in his own day.

PROPHECY AND THE PROPHETS 115

In point of fact, however, there is a real connection. In the period of the early monarchy we find prophets who undoubtedly had a real message from Yahweh, while in the later prophets, even the greatest, we find hints that earlier "ecstatic" elements survived. Right through the books of Samuel and Kings we find records of men who spoke the word of God to make his will known—Samuel himself, Nathan who seems to have taken over Samuel's rôle as kingmaker (1 Kings 1) as well as rebuking David for sin (2 Sam. 12. 1-15), Ahijah (1 Kings 11. 29ff), Micaiah ben Imlah (1 Kings 22. 5ff), and others. The most important here are, of course, Elijah and Elisha, about both of whom considerable cycles of stories have been preserved. The picture of Elijah has much in common both with the "seer" and with the "ecstatic". He runs before Ahab's chariot from Carmel to Jezreel (1 Kings 18. 46), and spends much of his time in the desert, coming into the settled area only for special purposes. (In this he seems to have much in common with the Nazirites (see Num. 6. 1-21; Judges 13. 5, 7; Amos 2. 11, 12) and the Rechabites (see Jer. 35. 5-10).) Yet his message is clearly a word from Yahweh, and like that of Samuel and the later prophets it is directed towards the social and religious sins of the nation, especially those of the monarch. Elisha is a rather more shadowy figure, but he, too, acts as king maker and deposer (2 Kings 9), yet is a seer (2 Kings 6. 15ff; cf. 2. 9ff), and is inspired with music to prophesy (2 Kings 3. 15).

When we look at the prophets whom we know as the "writing" prophets, we seem to be in a different world. Amos, for instance, expressly disclaims connection with the type of prophet known in his time (7. 14, cf. 2 Kings 2. 3). At first sight, it seems that we are dealing with preachers more or less as we know them to-day. Yet there are references which suggest that they had more in common with the ecstatics than we suppose. Hos. 9. 7 says, for instance:

> The prophet is a fool,
> the man of the spirit is mad.

Jeremiah at times acts under an inner compulsion which affects him physically as well as mentally (4. 19-21; 23. 9), while in a number of his experiences, Ezekiel acts in a way which certainly seems abnormal (3. 26; 4. 4-8; 6. 11; 20. 45-7). Although to us the distinction between these men and those also known as "prophets" at the time seems quite clear, it was by no means so clear to their contemporaries. They seemed to be a few among many using more or less the same methods, and claiming the same attention.[1] There was confusion as to what did or did not make a man a prophet, and how true prophets were to be distinguished from false (see Deut. 18. 20-2; Jer. 28. 9). The test suggested was not, however, ideal. Jeremiah himself was considered a false prophet (11. 21), and even if the test proved valid, it was a little late to discover whether a warning was true or not after the event has happened! (See pp. 117-19, below.)

We see the prophets, then, as very varied types. On the one hand, the "ecstatic" whose message is given in a frenzy which suggests to some onlookers the direct control of Yahweh, but to others may seem quite meaningless; at the other extreme a truly inspired, intelligible message given by the great prophets. No doubt there were many whose activities were of both kinds, and we should be foolish to think that only those men whose words have come down to us were truly men of God giving his message to the people. Nor should we be worried about "ecstatic" elements in the great prophets (though scholars dispute the extent of this). Our concern must be first and foremost with the source of the message and its content rather than with the method of its delivery. Modern psychological studies have thrown a

---

[1] Cf. Jeremiah 28, where he and Hananiah contend together using almost identical words and actions.

good deal of light on the way in which ideas and beliefs deeply held may be brought up from the subconscious even when a man is apparently beside himself—it may even be that this is the greatest "moment of truth". Now the prophet is essentially a man living a life based on Yahweh: he seeks his will in all things, and desires to bring others to know what he will have them do. Such a man comes so much closer to God than others that his knowledge of him and his ways is far deeper, and from this knowledge comes his message. To put it another way, the prophet seeking to do the will of God is so inspired by God that he begins to look at the world through God's eyes, and so is enabled to communicate a "word" from Yahweh to his people. This message is so much a part of the prophet that it really makes very little difference whether it is transmitted in a state of ecstasy or one of full consciousness. In view of the fact that in the ancient world, as in modern nomadic Arab society, the madman was considered specially inspired by God, we shall hardly be surprised to find ecstasy as the normal method of prophetic activity. God, if we may put it so, uses human agents to transmit his message in the way most acceptable to those for whom it is intended.

This still leaves us without an answer to the question of how to distinguish between true prophecy and false. It is not necessary for us to consider false prophecy as deliberate imposture. A great deal can come from the subconscious, and it is fatally easy to mistake the imaginations of our own minds for the promptings of God. It is true that Micah (3. 5) condemns those who give a pleasant message to those who pay them, but "declare war" against those who do not; but this does not mean deliberate hypocrisy.[2] But it still remains a problem to distinguish the true from the false, a problem

[2] We have all read of twentieth-century clergymen with a good deal to say about the iniquities of those who do not support Church funds.

felt by the Israelite as much as by us. For him, the problem was essentially practical, as for instance in 1 Kings 22. Here Ahab and Jehoshaphat had to decide which prophetic message to accept, and the fate of Ahab shows the advisability (to put it no more strongly!) of making a correct choice. A similar problem arose when Jeremiah and Hananiah clashed (Jer. chs. 27 and 28). That there was a continual temptation for the prophet to give a "popular" message can hardly be doubted (Mic. 3. 11; Isa. 30. 10; Jer. 5. 31; 14. 15ff; 23. 9-32), and no doubt many were prepared to give heed only to those things which suited them (a fact well known to fortune tellers to-day). But what of those who really were seeking the word of the Lord? How were they to decide?

The Book of Deuteronomy gives two tests: fulfilment (18. 21, 22) and content (13. 1-5; 18. 20). Both are blunt weapons. There could have been few who gave the message "worship other Gods", while in the case of Micaiah ben Imlah, for instance, the message was certainly vindicated by fulfilment, but rather late! Ahab would no doubt have preferred to have had a surer test capable of earlier application. It was, moreover, a test which could discredit the true prophet. Jeremiah, for instance, suffered neglect and persecution because of the non-fulfilment of his message of woe. People looked for immediate fulfilment, and did not take the long view. How could they? The fact is, of course, that there is no immediate means of saying what is and what is not a message from God. It is true that the genuine message will not contain something which is clearly against the truth of God, but to test a message simply by its conformity to accepted ideas will ensure stagnation and lack of progress. The only real tests which can be applied are the response which the message evokes at the time, and the authentication of history. Although the former is necessary, for without it the message would not be preserved and handed on,[3] only the second is infallible. The decisive question is, "Was the message accepted by later Israelites, in the light of historical perspective and their own greater knowledge of the ways of Yahweh, as a true revelation of his will?" It is the answer "Yes" to this question which led to the inclusion of the prophetic writings in the Old Testament Canon as part of the record of the Covenant people.

DETACHED NOTE:
PROPHECY AND THE CULTUS

In some ways the prophet was cut off from, and stood in opposition to, the general life of the nation. He came from outside with a message to the people, and went off again into nowhere. The typical example is Elijah. In particular we may point out the way in which many of the prophets seem to have been in opposition to the cultus as practised at the great sanctuaries. (E.g. Amos 4. 4, 5; Hos. 6. 6; Isa. 1. 11-15. Many other references could be quoted.) Nevertheless, there are difficulties in the view which would draw a clear line of opposition between prophecy and the cult.

In the first place, there were many "genuine" prophets who were closely connected with the sanctuaries. Samuel, for instance, besides being the best-known prophet of his day, seems to have been almost what later ages would have called "High Priest". Nathan is closely connected with the Jerusalem sanctuary, and joins with Zadok the priest in anointing Solomon (1 Kings 1. 32-40). Ahijah works at Shiloh (1 Kings 11. 29; 14. 2). Among the "writing" prophets, Ezekiel was himself a priest (Ezek. 1. 3) and Jeremiah at least came from a priestly family (Jer. 1. 1, though since this was not the Jerusalem priesthood, and

[3] Though the response may come only from a very few.

his work was almost entirely done in that city, perhaps we ought not to make too much of this), and did a good deal of his work in the Temple (7. 2ff; 19. 14ff; 24. 1; 26. 2; 36. 5, 6; etc.). Isaiah received his call while in the Temple, probably during an actual offering of sacrifice (Isa. 6. 1-7). These examples alone would suggest that the division between prophet and priest was not so deep as is sometimes suggested. In addition, it has been observed that there is a good deal of overlap between Psalms and the prophetic material: as Psalms is especially cultic material this is significant.

The psalms naturally include elements of praise, prayer, and thanksgiivng. The characteristic utterance of the prophet is, "Thus says the LORD", and the prophetic "I" is always God. We would not expect prophetic material of this kind in a hymn book, nor would we expect "psalm" material in a prophecy, unless there was close connection between the two forms of activity. Examples of such overlapping are, however, not uncommon. Ps. 81 is a good case. Verses 1 to 5a set the scene: God is being praised for his qualities on a solemn feast day, presumably Passover. In verse 5b a new note comes in: the "I" is clearly God, and this is a prophetic call to the nation to understand the implications of their deliverance. It almost looks as though a hymn being sung in a sanctuary was interrupted by a prophetic utterance so striking and apposite that it was remembered, retained for future exhortation, and eventually became part of the Psalm itself. Similar points may be seen in Ps. 95 (break at 7b), Ps. 50 (verses 7-15 inserted) and in other places. On the other hand, there are passages in the prophets which look suspiciously like "psalm" material. Hos. 6. 1-3 could almost find a place in the Psalter, and with the following verses provides a close parallel to Ps. 81. In Amos a number of passages long recognized on literary grounds as not being by Amos seem to be of this nature

PROPHECY AND THE CULTUS

(4. 13; 5. 8, 9;[4] 9. 5, 6). Mic. 7. 16-20 also seems similar. Once more it looks as though we have prophetic material originally spoken in the context of worship and preserved at the sanctuaries.

When we remember that there were bands of prophets at the great shrines (e.g. 2 Kings 2. 3, Bethel), that there was a "handing on" of prophetic office (e.g. 2 Kings 2. 9, 10), and that even the great prophets were "ecstatic" at times, the picture becomes clearer. It seems probable that the "great" prophets were simply the outstanding members of such prophetic guilds, especially those of the Jerusalem Temple, and that their words were handed down orally within the association until eventually committed to writing. This might happen quickly (cf. Jer. 36), or, probably much more often, after a longer time. When the longer period elapsed, it would be easy for other oracles in the same spirit by later members of the same guild to find their way into the cycle of tradition, and so into the final written form.[5] Such a development might well account, for instance, for the present form of the Book of Isaiah. Its three-fold division seems entirely justified on critical grounds, yet we have also to account for peculiarities of thought and expression which show the three parts to have much more in common with each other than with other prophetic literature. It is also a hypothesis which saves us postulating the enormously complicated process of editing and re-editing which is necessary if we think merely of literary activity, and which helps to clear up a number of obscurities of expression both in Psalms and the prophets.

Finally, it also helps us to see the life of Israel as a unity, centred on its worship. There has always been great diffi-

[4] The "seek him" of the English versions has, of course, no Hebrew equivalent.

[5] We remember that on literary grounds many of the prophetic books have to be considered composite documents.

culty in thinking of a religion in which its greatest creative force has been separated from its most characteristic actions, and from the main stream of religious life of the nation. Now we see the prophets as vitally concerned with the cultus: it is true that they condemn much of the way in which it was carried out and the motives which actuated many of those taking part; but their object is to make worship what it ought to be, and not to do away with it altogether.

THE TORAH

The usual translation of *torah* is "law". This is, however, a quite misleading translation, which leads to a quite false impression of the whole ethos of Judaism. The root from which the word is taken has the meaning "to point out" or "to direct", and the word itself means "direction", or perhaps "instruction". The idea that *torah* was a code of laws to be kept strictly in the most minute detail, is one which was held, no doubt, by some Pharisees, but it is confined to a small minority during a very brief period of history. It would have been quite impossible for Ps. 119 to have been written by a man who held this legalistic view of *torah*, and the whole Psalm well repays study by anyone who wants to know just what *torah* meant to a pious Jew.

Let us then look at the use of the word. It occurs frequently in Proverbs in the sense of "teaching", or even "advice for living" (e.g. 1. 8; 3. 1; 4. 2; 6. 22, 23; etc.). It is the knowledge of the ways of God which is found in the heart (Isa. 51. 7), or taught by the prophets (Zech. 7. 12; Jer. 26. 4, 5). In particular it covers authoritative legal decisions by a priest (Deut. 17. 8-12) or a judge (Ex. 18. 15-20, see pp. 158-9, below). Collections of such *toroth* consequently came to be made at the sanctuaries, eventually developing into the law-codes with which we are familiar, to which the name *torah* is applied. We must, therefore, think of *torah* as "the way of life" rather than as "law", and this is also how the Jew considers it. It is the basis of his whole culture, not in any rigid way, but as both formative and controlling.

When God reveals himself through *torah*, it means that in any given situation the whole Israelite tradition is being applied. If this situation is likely to recur, then the decision reached becomes itself part of the tradition. But *torah* is not a code which is fixed for evermore: it is a way of life which is capable of infinite expansion and application. In its own way the "Tradition of the Elders", which led some into legalistic ways (cf. Mark 7. 1ff) is an illustration of this principle. It was an attempt to apply *torah* to the whole of life in a society which was very different from what it had been in earlier ages. It is not *torah* itself which is bad; it is the attempt to provide infallible salvation by rigid adherence to a minute code of law which is bad. It is a fault of exegesis, however, to identify *torah* with such a code. Where *torah* is treated in this way by a Jew it is as much a perversion of the true spirit of Judaism as would be the attempt to use the Gospels in the same way by a Christian.

PERSONAL RELIGION

It is one of the fallacies of the modern world that religion is simply a matter of the relationship with God of each individual as an individual. It comes, therefore, somewhat as a shock to modern man to realize that in the ancient world generally, and Israel in particular, such a proposition would have been quite unacceptable, and for a large part of their history it would not even have been understood: religion was so much a part of social and community life that any attempt at divorce would have been quite impossible. Moreover, for the great majority of people during the greater part of the pre-exilic period (and indeed after), personal religion in the sense of individual communion with God would have meant nothing simply because it was no part of their spiritual lives or experience.

We have already touched on this problem in dealing with the growth of individualism (pp. 88-91, above), when we discussed the place of Jeremiah in the development of such individual religion. It has been said that he was the "founder of personal religion", and though undoubtedly he was the one who made the greatest advance, his work was only possible because of his Hebrew background. Moreover, while it is true that in no earlier literature are there any parallels to the "Confessions" of Jeremiah (e.g. 12. 1ff; 20. 7ff), we should be foolish to argue that therefore no man earlier had similar experiences. On the contrary, when we consider that many earlier leaders of Israel had received their commissions in much the same way as Jeremiah, we shall probably come to think that in all probability some, at least, did share his experiences, even if they wrote down nothing about them. This will become clearer if we analyse the basic elements of Jeremiah's teaching:

i. That God has a call, which cannot be escaped.

ii. That God will give him strength to fulfil his will.

iii. That in spite of all appearances to the contrary, God is in control, and will vindicate his servant in due time.

iv. That God hears the prayers of those who call on him.

v. That it is the will of God that all men should have personal knowledge of his ways, and should not have to rely on prophet or priest for instruction.

In considering the earlier history of these ideas, we shall not at present consider the Psalms. There these ideas are expressed over and over again, but the composite nature of

PERSONAL RELIGION 125

the book, and a good deal of uncertainty about dates for many of the psalms,[6] make it difficult to use for this purpose. We shall, therefore, consider the Psalms separately.

Working backwards from Jeremiah, what do we see? In Isaiah, the call of the prophet is found in chapter 6. Here we have the call and its acceptance, and the assurance of strength to perform the work. Isaiah is assured that in spite of opposition God will be his strength (8. 11ff), and will vindicate his words (7. 10ff). Amos, too, is conscious of the individual call and support of Yahweh (7. 15), which cannot be refused (3. 8). Elijah pours out his complaint to God, and is conscious of his personal presence and guidance (1 Kings 19. 4, 9ff). He, too, is convinced that the power of God is behind him and his works (1 Kings 17. 1, etc.). In these earlier traditions, we shall not expect to find any details of the spiritual struggles of the men concerned, for we are dealing with narrative material and not autobiography. But when we consider, for instance, the call and response of Samuel (1 Sam. 3), David's repentance (2 Sam. 12. 7-23), Solomon's prayer for wisdom (1 Kings 3. 4ff), it will be clear that though the prayers of Jeremiah stand at a deeper level of intensity, they are not isolated from the Israelite tradition, which goes back even to Moses. We note his call and response (Ex. 3), his complaint at the commands and leadings of God (32. 11ff), and the personal relationship with God which comes out all through the narrative and which fully justifies the comment of the Deuteronomic editor that Moses was the one whom "the LORD knew face to face" (Deut. 34. 10).

We shall be less surprised at the paucity of material in the early narratives when we look at the post-Jeremiah part of the Old Testament. We have similar patterns of call and

[6] One of the difficulties is that one of the criteria for judging the date of a psalm is the relationship of that psalm to the subject we are discussing.

response in Ezekiel, with the assurance of support in rejection (Ezek. chs. 2 and 3): the story of Jonah (4. 1ff) shows that the author was familiar with prayer as dialogue between the individual and God (although it must be said that the content of the prayer is at a much lower level than that of Jeremiah). We find recorded prayers of Ezra (Ezra 9. 5ff; Neh. 9. 6ff), but even a superficial look at these will show that they are more in the nature of liturgical formulae than personal prayers. It would be easy to deduce from this that the post-exilic period forsook the piety of Jeremiah for an arid liturgical formalism. Such a conclusion would, however, take no account of the insights shown by the narratives in Daniel (e.g. 6. 10), the Prayer of Manasses in the Apocrypha, or in particular of the teachings and prayers of the Psalms. Whatever we may think of their possible origins, these were undoubtedly in use during the period of the Second Temple, and played a large part in the ritual of both Temple and synagogue. They were words which were familiar to every Israelite, and not only expressed the piety of ordinary men and women, but moulded it, even down to the present day.

The Book of Psalms is concerned both with private devotion and with public ceremony. It has been called the "hymn book of the Second Temple"; this is justified, but only if we remember that our English hymn books, too, have provided material not only for use in public worship, but for individual prayers.[7] They have grown into the religious life of those who use them. In the same way, the Psalms are part of the life of Israel. Some are particularly suited for great corporate occasions, others for the prayer of the closet. Yet all, no doubt, were used corporately, just

---

[7] Often enough it is the words of well-known and loved hymns which provide the most-used prayers for many, and are most asked for in times of trouble, as any minister who has assisted at a sick-bed or death-bed will testify.

PERSONAL RELIGION 127

as many of the most personal and intimate of our present-day hymns are sung with great fervour in Church, while all, no doubt, formed the raw material of the meditations of pious Jews. This dual nature of the book reminds us that Judaism never became a hot-house, forcing individual piety, but was the seed bed of a devotion informed and controlled by the living faith of the whole community, and nourished by the corporate worship of the Temple and (especially outside Jerusalem) the synagogue.

In Ps. 73 we see a man striving to understand what is beyond him, and finding the answer with God; though this is not itself a prayer, there can be little doubt that this describes an experience very like that of Jeremiah. Again, who can doubt that though it is composed in majestic language, Ps. 51 derives from an experience of sin, confession, and forgiveness so deep that it has acted as a "model" confession for all generations since? Ps. 22 shows a man experiencing utter dereliction, and yet through it all retaining his faith and trust in God. Ps. 42 and 43 are the plaint of a man cut off from the Temple and its worship, yet convinced that God has not cast him off but will deliver him and bring him once more to worship at God's altar. Anyone familiar with the Psalms will know how often phrases from them express exactly what the soul wants to say to its God, and how they speak to man's spiritual condition in all its aspects. Often enough the Psalms are condemned for use in public worship because their language and ideas are so foreign to those of to-day. This is, we may think, not because the Psalms are alien and outdated, but because the men of to-day have not, for the most part, that depth of spiritual life which alone can make the Psalms meaningful. The man who truly strives with God will find that they give him all that he needs, and more also. It is no accident that the Psalms have become an integral part of the liturgical and mystical heritage of Christianity, for it is in them that the spiritual life of Israel is found at its best and deepest. They are eloquent testimony to the strength and vitality of Israelite piety.

THE SPIRIT OF GOD

The Spirit of God, the Holy Spirit, is for Christians the supreme way in which God communicates with his people, making himself known, giving strength and power, and guiding his people. But the concept of the Spirit is not just a New Testament idea; its roots lie back in Old Testament thought, where, too, the Spirit was seen as one of the main ways in which God was active.

We have discussed the word *ruach* as it is applied to men in the section on "Man and his Make-up" (pp. 84-6, above). When applied to God, the Spirit is seen in action particularly:

  i. as the creative spirit, propagating and sustaining life;
  ii. as the source of the virtues in man;
  iii. in connection with the work of Messiah;

Finally, we shall see how in the Spirit is communicated the very presence of God himself.

The *locus classicus* for (i) *the creative spirit, propagating and sustaining life,* is, of course, Genesis 1. 2, where the Spirit of God is said to be present at the initial act of creation. The same conjunction of Spirit and Creative Word is found in Ps. 33. 6:

> By the word of the LORD the heavens were made,
>   and all their host by the breath (*ruach*) of his mouth.

and in particular the Spirit is concerned with the creation of sentient beings:

> When thou sendest forth thy Spirit, they are created;
>   and thou renewest the face of the ground.   (Ps. 104. 30)

especially man:

THE SPIRIT OF GOD

> The spirit (*ruach*) of God has made me,
> and the breath of the Almighty gives me life. (Job 33. 4)

and not only creation, but also continuing care. This is seen in the way in which the Spirit is (ii) *the source of all virtues in man*. In particular, the Spirit is the source of all intellectual activities:

> . . . the Spirit of the LORD shall rest upon him,
> the spirit of wisdom and understanding,
> the spirit of counsel and might,
> the spirit of knowledge and the fear of the LORD. (Isa. 11. 2)

> But it is the spirit (*ruach*) in a man,
> the breath (*neshamah*) of the Almighty,
> that makes him understand. (Job 32. 8)

It is the Spirit that gives insight into the meaning of revelations (Gen. 41. 38), skill in artistic workmanship (Ex. 31. 2-5), and skill in making vestments for the priests (Ex. 28. 3, where R.S.V. "an able mind" is, literally, "a spirit of wisdom"). It is the inspiration of the Judges especially for waging war against the enemies of Israel (Judges 3. 10; 6. 34; 11. 29, etc.). It is also given that Israel may be judged (Num. 11. 17), and to the one who is to have authority over the people (Num. 27. 18). In short, any out of the ordinary activity of this kind is the result of the activity of the Spirit of God.

The Spirit is also the source of inspiration. We may well understand ecstatic prophecy to be the gift of the Spirit (cf. 1 Sam. 10. 6; 19. 20, etc.), but Spirit inspiration is not confined to such violent manifestations, but is seen in others who teach what they are taught by God (e.g. Balaam, Num. 24. 2), and, by a natural transition, in all prophecy:

> . . . as for me, I am filled with power,
> with the Spirit of the LORD . . .
> to declare to Jacob his transgression
> and to Israel his sin. (Mic. 3. 8)

See also Ezek. 11. 1, etc. It is the Spirit which inspires the Servant of the Lord (Isa. 42. 1), and also the Psalmist:

> The oracle of David, the son of Jesse . . .
>   the sweet psalmist of Israel:
> "The Spirit of the LORD speaks by me,
>   his word is upon my tongue . . . " (2 Sam. 23. 1, 2)

while the Spirit is the giver of all wisdom (cf. Wis. 9. 17; 7. 22ff, etc.)

As we would expect, therefore, it is the Spirit which is the source of the moral and religious life of men:

> Create in me a clean heart, O God,
>   and put a new and right spirit (*ruach*) within me.
> Cast me not away from thy presence,
>   and take not thy holy Spirit (*ruach*) from me. (Ps. 51, 10, 11)

That is to say, the *ruach* of God strives with the *ruach* of man, in order that man may be what God intends him to be. In particular, it enables men to walk according to the commands of Yahweh:

> And I will put my spirit within you, and cause you to walk in my statutes and be careful to observe my ordinances.
> (Ezek. 36. 27)

With this passage should be taken Ezekiel's vision of the Valley of Dry Bones in 37. 1-14, in which the restoration of Israel to a truly living nation is seen as the work of the wind/Spirit.

It is the Spirit which leads individuals in the right way:

> Teach me to do thy will,
>   For thou art my God!
> Let thy good spirit lead me
>   on a level path. (Ps. 143. 10)

and leads to deepening of compassion, and mourning because of wrong-doing:

And I will pour out on the house of David and the inhabitants
of Jerusalem a spirit of compassion and supplication, so that,
when they look on him whom they have pierced, they shall
mourn for him . . .   (Zech. 12. 10)

It is, then, the Spirit which inspires men to do the will
and purpose of God. Since the Messianic age is primarily
the time when God's will will be done in earth, it is hardly
surprising that we find the Spirit (iii) *closely connected with
the Messiah*.

The best-known passages are, of course, Isa. 61. 1ff and
11. 1ff, in both of which the Spirit is seen as the inspirer of
God's chosen one. (The former passage is also quoted by
Jesus with reference to his own ministry, Luke 4. 16ff.) One
of the signs of the Messianic age will be a general pouring
forth of the Spirit (Joel 2. 28f). The passage quoted above
from Ezek. 36 is part of the prophet's description of the
work of Yahweh in recreating the nation. In general, therefore, when Israel comes under the full sovereignty of God,
then the work of the Spirit will be particularly apparent.

It has been clear from a number of passages already
quoted that the active presence of the Spirit is the presence
of God himself (Ps. 51. 11; 143. 10). The Spirit and the
presence of God are put in parallel in Ps. 139. 7 :

Whither shall I go from thy Spirit?
   Or whither shall I flee from thy presence?

While in Hag. 2. 4, 5, we have :

   . . . I am with you, says the LORD of hosts . . . My Spirit abides
   among you . . .

Isa. 63. 7ff recounts the wonderful words of God at the
Exodus, and in several places it is the Spirit that is seen to
be active (vv. 10. 11, 14). It is true that there are several
passages (e.g. Isa. 34. 16; 48. 16) in which the Spirit seems
half-personalized into a separate identity. But this is only a

literary form; there is no idea of a separate "person" of the Spirit. Rather, where the Spirit is, there is God himself active in all his ways.

WORSHIP, SACRIFICE, AND PRIESTHOOD

So far, we have been considering the way in which God communicates with man. The opposite activity, man's response, comes first of all, of course, in willing acceptance and obedience. But it is also seen, in a most characteristic way, in the worship which he offers, and it is this which we shall consider in this section.

The worship of a nation depends on its beliefs and theology, however unformed or unexpressed. Indeed, one of the best ways of getting to know what a people *really* believes is to examine closely its liturgy. Cultus is the real religious life of the nation. From our point of view, one of the main difficulties is that we have for the early period no detailed account of the forms taken by worship, and have to reconstruct what happened from isolated hints. For the later period, material is more abundant, but even so it is part of what was a living tradition, so that a good deal is taken for granted because it was so familiar, and thus difficulties arise.[8]

We have hardly any information of the worship of Israel in the nomadic period, prior to the entry into Canaan. The account of the making and furnishing of the sanctuary, and the directions for worship, as they are found in the Pentateuch, although ascribed to Moses, in fact reflect conditions and practice of a later period. It is possible to reconstruct to some extent by comparison with

[8] In the same way it would be extremely difficult, if not impossible, for anyone who had never attended a Church of England service to reconstruct what happens merely from an examination of the Book of Common Prayer.

WORSHIP, SACRIFICE, AND PRIESTHOOD 133

the religious practices of other nomadic peoples in the same area,[9] and this can often give the clue to the interpretation of difficult passages. It seems probable, to say the least, that it was worship directed towards one God, Yahweh. It probably had among its cult-objects the ark and the brazen serpent, and included sacrifice as part of its ritual, certainly some form of "common meal" sacrifice (see pp. 150-1, below), and possibly some form of "gift" offering (see pp. 151-2, below). There were almost certainly special rites for specific times, probably almost all based on the lunar calendar—New Moons, Spring Festival, and probably the Sabbath. In all probability, certain places (e.g. Sinai/Horeb) were thought of as specially holy, although worship was not confined to them (cf. Ex. 20. 24, which suggests that Yahweh was to be worshipped wherever man was convinced of his presence: an example of the way this might happen is found in Gen. 28. 10-22). The form of worship was probably relatively simple and direct.

These are not certainties, only probabilities; beyond this, we are moving into the realm of speculation. It is, of course, quite otherwise with the worship of the settled peoples of the Fertile Crescent. Many religious texts and similar documents have been recovered, and temples excavated. We have therefore much more material for reconstructing the form which Israel's worship took after entry into Canaan and after assimilation of Canaanite forms.[10] As we have seen, a great deal of the growth in pre-exilic times was concerned with the purging out of these foreign elements and restoring the true Israelite tradition. In order, therefore, to see what the permanent elements are, we shall look most particularly at the worship of post-exilic Judaism,

[9] As, for example, with the Arab peoples, by W. Robertson Smith in *The Religion of the Semites* (1890). (The 3rd edition (revised) of 1927 should be used.)

[10] See pp. 55-8, above.

134 THE RELATIONS BETWEEN GOD AND MAN

remembering that a good deal was recent addition and accretion. Remembering that we are discussing the meeting of man with God, we shall try to answer four main questions:

i. Where could man meet God?
ii. On what occasions?
iii. What actions were necessary to bring about the meeting?[11]
iv. What intermediaries, if any, were necessary?

In other words: sanctuaries, festivals, sacrifice, and priesthood.

i. Sanctuaries

From the point of view of post-Exilic Judaism, seen in *Leviticus* and *Deuteronomy,* the place *par excellence* for sacrifice was the Jerusalem Temple. When other sanctuaries are mentioned, they are thought of as irregular. Such an estimate is found in the way in which Kings refers to the Northern sanctuaries at Dan and Bethel, and to the worship of the High places. Kings, however, is history written from the particular point of view of Southern scribes who accepted whole-heartedly the rule of the one sanctuary. Those who were living in the pre-Deuteronomic period would have been astounded to be told that in worshipping at sanctuaries other than Jerusalem they were sinning. It was natural to them, normal, and what had come down from leaders in the past.

The essence of a sanctuary was that it was a place where God had made himself known in the past (cf. Ex. 20. 24). It was not so much a place where God could be met as a place where God had been met once, and where therefore he was likely to be met again. The story of Jacob at Bethel

[11] And, therefore, how do these actions help us to understand the nature of the meeting?

(Gen. 28. 10-22) is a good illustration of the sort of theophany which started a sanctuary. In all probability this story was handed down at Bethel as a sort of "Foundation Document". Similarly, Gilgal (according to Josh. 4. 19—5. 9) became a sanctuary as a memorial of the power of Yahweh in bringing the nation over Jordan. In all probability, the history of such places goes back long before the time of the Hebrew invasions, or even the Patriarchs. Isolated, naturally occurring, stones are frequently sites for primitive sanctuaries (e.g. the natural stone at Jerusalem), while groups of standing stones are often relics of very ancient shrines (e.g. Stonehenge): the unusual is taken to be the mark of the presence of an abnormal—i.e. divine— being, and becomes a place of worship. Isolated trees, perhaps of peculiar shape, or remembered for some other reason, seem to have been cultic centres (Gen. 35. 4, 8; Josh. 24. 26; Judges 4. 5; 6. 11). So, too, were hilltops, perhaps marked by a tree, or by an artificial tree, the *asherah* (A.V. "grove"). Such "high places" were common, and references to them are frequent right through the historical books. Notice particularly 1 Kings 3. 2, 3, with the clear implication that not only was nothing wrong seen in worship there, but that Yahweh was firmly believed to appear at them. There can be little doubt that they were used by the Canaanites before the Hebrew invasions and taken over by the newcomers, together with most of their ritual. It is the latter point which causes the book of Deuteronomy to insist that there shall be only one sanctuary for Israel, echoing no doubt the teaching of the great prophets (Deut. 12. 1-14; cf. Hos. 4. 13-19; Mic. 5. 13, 14; etc). It was on the basis of Deuteronomy that Josiah carried out his great reform (2 Kings 23) including the centralization of worship at Jerusalem. The reform was short-lived, as is evident from such passages as Ezek. 6. 3, 4, but the reversion also did not last long, for in less than thirty years the worship of Yahweh had ceased altogether in Palestine, with the carrying away of the leaders, including the priests, to Babylonia.

It is the Exile which really brings matters to a head. There, they were cut off entirely from all sanctuaries, and if some older ideas had been retained, were cut off from Yahweh himself.[12] But two things happened. First, the Jerusalem priesthood was prominent among the leaders in Babylonia. As they prepared for the return they collected and codified their traditions, naturally emphasizing the law of the one sanctuary at Jerusalem. Closer knowledge of pagan worship made them even more eager than before to make sure that no such practices would ever again contaminate Israel. So it was that when the people returned, it was to build the Jerusalem Temple as the sole sanctuary of Yahweh. This was made easier by the second development. Although absence from their own land had made sacrificial worship impossible, the exiles retained their national identity, and met together for religious purposes. We hear of prophetic activity (cf. Ezek. 13) and no doubt the Psalms were used (in spite of Ps. 137). It was a time of intense literary activity, with the collection of the traditions, history, and customs of the people: this material would have been read in order to keep alive the knowledge of the nation that had once been, and would surely live again. So began that form of non-sacrificial worship which was to develop into the synagogue. When, therefore, the exiles returned those too far away from Jerusalem for regular worship in the Temple did not feel the need for local sanctuaries, but maintained synagogues instead. They were, of course, a necessary feature of Judaism in the Dispersion, and remain so to-day.

[12] For the idea that the God of Israel could be worshipped only on Israelite soil see e.g. 1 Sam. 26. 19; 2 Kings 5. 17.

WORSHIP, SACRIFICE, AND PRIESTHOOD

There was just one exception that we know of: the Temple at Elephantine, near Aswan in Upper Egypt. Nothing is said of this in the Old Testament, but in 1908 excavations at the site resulted in the discovery of a large number of papyrus documents which had originated in the fifth century B.C. They came from a Jewish community there, and amongst a mass of secular material, there are some which throw light on its religious life. They had a Temple where worship was offered to Yahweh, under the name "Yahu".[13] Alongside Yahu, however, others were worshipped, including a goddess, Anath-Yahu, who seems to have been regarded as a consort of Yahu, and a series of Gods whose names are compounded with Bethel—Ishum-Bethel, Cherem-Bethel, Anath-Bethel (cf. Gen. 31. 13, and Jer. 48. 13, where Bethel is parallel to Chemosh the god of Moab). The origin of this community is not known, but there can be little doubt that this Temple preserved a great deal of normal pre-exilic practice. It is hardly surprising that relations with Jerusalem were not of the best! What happened to it eventually is not known. We have just this one picture from the fifth century, and that is all.

One other post-exilic sanctuary may be mentioned—that of the Samaritans on Mount Gerizim. It is most probable that it was built towards the end of the fourth century, and its erection made permanent the split between Jews and Samaritans. It is referred to in the New Testament (John 4, esp. vv. 9 and 20). Although the prescriptions of the Law were carried out, it was never accepted by the Jews as a legitimate place of sacrifice. Accordingly it escaped the destruction of A.D. 70, and the tiny Samaritan community still living near Nablus still offers sacrifice on Mount Gerizim.

---

[13] It is possible, though in the opinion of many scholars unlikely, that this was the original form of the name we transliterate as "Yahweh".

In the later Old Testament period, the overwhelming majority of Jews worshipped regularly in synagogue, visits to the Jerusalem Temple being more in the nature of pilgrimage.[14] This was true even among those resident in Jerusalem itself where there were many synagogues (cf. Acts 6. 9). The word "synagogue" originally indicated an assembly of the people, particularly an assembly for worship; it soon became attached to the place or building used for assemblies. But the synagogue was not merely a place of worship: it was the school, where Jewish boys were taught to read and write (especially the Scriptures), and the place where legal decisions were taken, disputes settled, and the law upheld (cf. Matt. 10. 17). There are records of its use for political debate, and as a hostel for travellers. It was, in fact, the centre of all Jewish community life. This did not detract from its use as a place of worship. Rather, it bears witness to the Jewish insight that worship is a vital part of all life, and not merely one aspect of it. It is true that this may lead to abuse, as for example in the Temple (cf. Mark 11. 15ff, etc.), but abuse does not mean that there is not real insight also.

ii. *The occasions of worship*

There are three main groups of occasions for worship:
(a) The regular corporate religious activities of the community.
(b) The hallowing of great national (irregular) events.
(c) The hallowing of personal (irregular) events.

In the present day these give us (a) the regular day by day and week by week worship of congregations, (b) such activities as Coronation, National Days of Prayer or Thanksgiving, State Marriages or Funerals, etc., and (c) personal activities such as Baptism, Thanksgiving after

[14] Much as a modern Moslem tries to make the Mecca pilgrimage once in his lifetime.

WORSHIP, SACRIFICE, AND PRIESTHOOD   139

Childbirth, Marriage, etc., events which have been hallowed in all religions from the earliest times.

a. *The regular, corporate religious activities of the community*

This may be sub-divided again into the keeping of Festivals, and the "workaday" observances. The major national festivals are those of Passover (*Pesach*), Tabernacles or Booths (*Succoth*), Pentecost or Weeks (*Chag Shabu'oth*), and the Day of Atonement (*Yom hakkippurim*); there are also the lesser feasts of Purim and Dedication, and others of interest only to those who keep them and to the specialist. Purim is connected now with the story of the Book of Esther, although whether this was its origin is doubtful; it is a happy and cheerful feast, a time of general rejoicing. Dedication commemorates the rededication of the Temple by Judas Maccabaeus after its pollution by Antiochus Epiphanes (1 Macc. 4. 52-9; 2 Macc. 10. 1-8; cf. John 10. 22). The main "workaday" observances are New Moon and Sabbath. We are concerned here with the significance of these feasts in historical Israel rather than with origins, and it is sufficient therefore to note that they go right back to the earliest days of the nation, linking up with the normal activities of nomadic peoples all over the Fertile Crescent, being both lunar feasts.

The most important of the Festivals was Passover. In its historic form it is essentially the commemoration of the deliverance from Egypt, although its origins clearly go back to two separate rites—a nomadic spring festival connected with a lamb, and an agricultural observance connected with the unleavened bread. It was one of the occasions when all males were to "appear before Yahweh" (Ex. 23. 14, 15). The central features of the rite were the slaying of the lamb, the sprinkling of its blood, and the eating of its flesh. With it is associated the eating of unleavened bread for seven days (Deut. 16. 1-8). The lamb is eaten under the same conditions as those supposed to have accompanied the original Exodus (Ex. 12. 11). In this sense, it is a re-creation of the original situation : those taking part are identifying themselves with the Israelites in Egypt, and with the salvation wrought then by Yahweh. The Deuteronomic code provides that Passover shall be kept only at Jerusalem, a new requirement (2 Kings 23. 21-3), associated with the centralization of all sacrifice. Consequently the present-day celebration of Passover is, as it were, a substitute for the sacrificial rite. Even so, a look at the ritual prescribed will show that it is still very much a re-enactment of the acts of God's original salvation, together with an anticipation of future blessing by which Israel will once more be led out of dispersion to their own land. This is thoroughly in line with Old Testament ideas about the significance of the feast.

Tabernacles was originally the climax of the agricultural year, celebrating the completion of harvest. The "booths" in which it is kept are reckoned by Israel to represent the tents used in the wilderness period. It now comes in the seventh month of the year, but originally seems to have corresponded with general practice in the Fertile Crescent and have been closely connected with New Year (Ex. 34. 22, "the feast of ingathering at the year's end"). In origin clearly what we should call a "Harvest Thanksgiving", it is now, like Passover, reinterpreted as an enactment of the events of salvation connected with the Exodus.

Pentecost (Weeks) comes seven weeks after Passover (Deut. 16. 9ff; Lev. 23. 9ff). In origin commemorating the completion of the corn harvest begun at Passover, by the later Jews and at the present day it commemorates the giving of the Law on Mount Sinai.

Closely connected with Tabernacles is the Fast of the Day of Atonement. We shall consider the ritual of this day

WORSHIP, SACRIFICE, AND PRIESTHOOD 141

when we look at the significance of sacrifice (pp. 148-56, below). Here we notice that it comes just before Tabernacles, i.e. New Year (Num. 29. 7-11). It is clearly a post-Exilic institution,[15] for it finds no mention in Deuteronomy, and is not found in biblical literature outside the Pentateuch except in Ecclus. 50. 5ff. The idea, however, is quite clear. During the year, almost certainly, there have accumulated sins for which, by ignorance or inadvertence, the requisite sin- or guilt-offering have not been made; in order that there may be a fresh start to the New Year there is, on this day, a solemn cleansing of the whole people, by which atonement is made for all so far unatoned sins. It is hardly necessary to say that it is not intended for, and has no significance for, sins committed "with a high hand".

Of the "workaday" observances, two stand out as particularly observed in Old Testament times—New Moon and Sabbath. New Moon is clearly in origin a festival connected with a lunar cult: the ritual is found in Num. 10. 10 and 28. 11-15 (both P). It is mentioned a number of times in the prophetic literature (1 Sam. 20. 5, 24; Isa. 1. 13, 14; Amos 8. 5) and in Ps. 81. 3, 4. Little is known of it except that it was a time of rejoicing and a holy day. Ex. 40. 2, 17 may suggest that it was connected in some way with a commemoration of the raising of the tabernacle, though it is equally possible that the nature of the observance has influenced this passage. Sabbath also has a very obscure origin. It, too, is clearly connected with the phases of the moon, and in Amos and Isaiah is mentioned in close connection with New Moon. It is found very early on, and almost certainly goes back to the origins of the nation. Ex. 20. 11 justifies it as a commemoration of creation, a view reflected in the P creation story (Gen. 2. 1-3). We have also, however, the Deuteronomic interpretation (Deut.

---

[15] Though cf. pp. 153-5, below.

5. 15) that it commemorates the deliverance from Egypt. The way in which the command is given in both versions of the Ten Words shows that it was already a known observance. In the pre-exilic period it does not seem to have been marked by the rigid requirements of the later time. There is certainly a prohibition of trade (Amos 8. 5, where New Moon is subject to the same restriction), and at the same time both New Moon and Sabbath are particularly auspicious occasions for consulting a man of God (2 Kings 4. 23). Sabbath was also a day when large numbers came together for worship (2 Kings 11. 4-16). It is essentially a day for remembering God's blessings and salvation, to be thought of not as a burden but a delight (Isa. 58. 13, 14). It is a continual re-entering into God's salvation, a memorial which finds moments of climax in the great festivals when the events of redemption are eloquently proclaimed in word and ritual.

b. The hallowing of great national events

These are almost always connected with the King. This is quite understandable: in Fertile Crescent culture, the king was the focus of the life of the nation. At any event of national importance, he automatically took first place; conversely, any event connected with the king *was* an event of national importance.

It has been suggested that in the period of the monarchy one of the major events of the year was a New Year Festival not dissimilar to that found in the religions of Egypt, Babylonia, and Canaan. In this ritual, the king took the part of the God, and with appropriate words and ceremony was enthroned as king, took part in a mock combat with one representing his enemies, and consummated a sacred marriage with one acting the part of the goddess. The purpose of this ritual was to ensure that in the coming year God would indeed remain supreme over his people, would

WORSHIP, SACRIFICE, AND PRIESTHOOD 143

vanquish all their enemies, and with the goddess would give fertility to ground and animals. The evidence for the existence of such a ritual in Israel is almost entirely indirect (it is hardly likely that post-Exilic editors would retain material with such obvious pagan affinities!), and is strongly disputed by many scholars. It is impossible to go into the pros and cons of the problem in this short work, and readers interested should consult the volumes edited by S. H. Hooke in defence,[16] and against it that by N. H. Snaith.[17]

Of other events connected with the king, by far the most important was the coronation. No instructions for this (or indeed any other royal occasions) have come down to us: no doubt the editors of the Pentateuch felt that they were unnecessary in a situation where there was no king, and where his functions were carried out by the High Priest. It is quite clear, however, that some of the Psalms (Pss. 2, 21, 72, 110 at least) were used on that occasion, and we also have accounts of what took place in parts of the historical books (1 Kings 1. 32-40, Solomon; 2 Kings 11. 11, 12, Joash). There are a number of important points which arise from these about the nature and significance of the coronation ceremony.

The term "coronation" is misleading. The central act was the anointing with oil, in much the same way as the High Priest (cf. Ex. 30. 22ff). The crown has very little to do with it.[18] Psalm 110 will help us in seeing the function of the

---

[16] *Myth and Ritual* (Oxford 1933), The Labyrinth (S.P.C.K. 1935), *Myth, Ritual and Kingship* (Oxford 1958).

[17] *The Jewish New Year Festival* (S.P.C.K. 1948).

[18] Both ceremonies—anointing and coronation—are found in the modern coronation ritual, and although the coronation is now the climax of the ceremony, the anointing is the really important part. The monarch is not anointed as a preparation for a coronation: he is crowned as a consequence of being anointed.

king. He was "an eternal priest after the order of Melchisedech." Melchisedech was, of course, the Jebusite Priest-King of Jerusalem (Gen. 14)—we have, incidentally, the clear implication that a good deal more was taken over from the Jebusites than their town—and an Israelite king after the same order was clearly not only ruler but also priest *par excellence* of the nation. It is he who offers sacrifice on great national occasions, as for instance in 2 Sam. 6 (the whole chapter, but especially verses 17 and 18) and 1 Kings 8. If we compare 2 Kings 15. 1-7 with the later parallel narrative of the Chronicler (2 Chron. 26. 16ff) we see how the tradition of the royal priesthood has given way to the post-exilic idea of an Aaronic High Priest. In the same passages we also see the King performing the priestly function of blessing.

There is no interval between accession and coronation. To-day, coronation is a great spectacle which needs months of preparation, during which time the sovereign has been exercising all royal functions. Such delay was impossible in Israel, for in a very real sense the king was essential to the life of the nation. Until the king had been anointed, he was not the nation's priest, he was not their intermediary with God, so that in a very real way the nation thought of itself as separated from God. The interval between the death of the old king and the accession of the new had to be as short as possible.[19] This sheds a good deal of light on the vision of Isaiah (Isa. 6), in which, during the interval between the death of Uzziah and the accession of Jotham, he saw Yahweh in the Temple, holy, and still the protector of his people.

In the same way, *prayers offered for the health, vigour, and long life of the king were much more than pious wishes.*

---

[19] Solomon, for instance, was anointed while David was still alive, though on his death bed (1 Kings 1).

WORSHIP, SACRIFICE, AND PRIESTHOOD 145

They were really meant, for the life and vigour of the nation were closely tied up with the health and vigour of the king. He was, in many ways, their embodiment as well as their mediator and representative.

Finally, we notice the way in which the king-nation relationship was *sealed with a covenant*. This has been dealt with earlier (see p. 46, above), and needs no further discussion here.

Since the king has this important function, it is clearly important that the royal line shall continue. The royal marriage was, therefore, an important event,[20] and we may note Ps. 45 in particular as a psalm used at a royal marriage.

c. The hallowing of personal events.

As in any community, the main events of this type were those connected the life and death—birth, puberty, marriage, and death. There were also the family sacrifices which took place year by year, and were much more a personal matter than part of the "official" cult (cf. 1 Sam. 1 and 2).

Of these, we know most about those connected with birth. The main points are those dealing with the mother—purification—and the child—circumcision. The purification ritual is found in Lev. 12. Basically, a woman who has borne a child is "unclean" for a fixed period, depending on the sex of the child, after which the sin-offering is brought together with a burnt-offering (as a thanksgiving). Ritual uncleanness connected with childbirth is extremely common in societies less civilized than our own,[21] and implies no

[20] Even more so if we hold that in Israel also ideas were held that the fruitfulness of the land depended on the sexual activities of the king, as in the sacred marriage of the New Year Festival referred to above.

[21] Though many relics of such beliefs still persist, as the writer (and no doubt many another priest) has found in parish life.

moral condemnation, nor that the processes involved in childbirth are sinful (as the term sin-offering might suggest). It simply means that for the period of uncleanness the mother is not allowed to take part in worship, and for part of the time at least will not come into contact with others. The offering at the end of the period is simply a ritual means of re-entering the worshipping community after absence. Also connected with this period is the *Redemption of the First-born* (Num. 18. 15f; Ex. 13. 12ff; 34. 19f; cf. Num. 3. 46ff). That this ceremony is a relic of the custom of offering first-born males as human sacrifice can hardly be doubted (the story of the saving of Isaac from death in Gen. 22 surely originated as authority for abrogation of the practice). In historic times only the first-born of those animals usually offered in sacrifice were actually killed; first-born of other animals, and especially humans, were "redeemed" by the offering of a substitute.

By far the most important of the birth ceremonies was circumcision. To-day, circumcision is almost entirely linked in our minds with Judaism, particularly since St Paul uses the word as almost the equivalent of "the Jewish faith". We need to remember that in the ancient world it was very much more common, and that it could hardly have been thought of as the distinctive mark of the Jews before the exile. In Palestine, other nations, too, used it with religious significance, and in the period of the monarchy and earlier it would have been difficult for it to have been thought of as particularly Jewish. We may be tempted, therefore, to consider it in the same way as did other nations, where it almost certainly acted as a sort of puberty sacrifice and ritual by which a boy was initiated into manhood. Adult circumcision was certainly used at times by Israel (cf. Josh. 5. 2ff), and was regularly practised with proselytes; but the Jewish custom is particularly *infant* circumcision, and so must have a different significance (it is probable that the

WORSHIP, SACRIFICE, AND PRIESTHOOD 147

story of Ex. 4. 24, 25 was originally told as authority for the custom). In Gen. 17. 9ff it is to be the sign of the covenant (P) and in Ex. 12. 48 (also P) it is commanded that no one uncircumcised shall eat the Passover: if a stranger wishes to do so, he must undergo the ceremony. When we remember that Passover is particularly the Exodus ceremony, it is clear that circumcision is intended to be the means of entry into the redeemed community. A similar idea is found in Josh. 5. 9, where it is said to symbolize that the reproach of Egypt has been rolled off.[22] In later times it was the occasion of the naming of the child, and took place on the eighth day after birth (cf. Luke 1. 59). Although in the New Testament, especially in Paul, the word is used almost as a term of reproach, Old Testament usage makes it clear that it was thought of as the outward symbol of a purified heart and obedience to God (cf. Deut. 10. 12-22, esp. v. 16).

We have mentioned puberty, and in many religions it is the occasion for a good deal of elaborate ceremony. There does not seem to have been the same emphasis in Judaism on the transition from childhood to adulthood—possibly because of the transfer of rites to infancy, as noted above. There are no regulations in the Pentateuch for such rites, nor are any such occasions found in the historical narrative.[23] We know that it was at twelve years of age that a Jewish boy first took part in the great festivals, and hence appropriated to himself the benefits of the Covenant (cf. Luke 2. 41, 42). At the present day, a Jewish boy becomes

[22] The connection of "rolling" with Gilgal is a piece of false etymology intended to explain the name Gilgal and its origins as a sanctuary. In all probability the story is the "foundation document" of Gilgal. But this does not invalidate the significance given to circumcision by the story.

[23] Unless the Isaac story of Gen. 22 is considered a "death and resurrection" myth connected with such an occasion (as in the later initiatory rituals of the Greek Mystery Religions), which does not seem probable.

Bar-Mitzvah (Son of the Commandment) by the ceremony of reading the *Torah* publicly in synagogue at the age of thirteen.

We may say almost the same of marriage; that it took place is obvious, and that it was thought to have both the sanction and blessing of God is clear. The high esteem in which it was held is widely attested. Yet no marriage rituals have come down from Old Testament times. In many ways this is something positive rather than negative. *Prima facie* we would expect the sort of rituals found in all early religions, to promote fertility and drive away evil spirits from the marriage bed. That such a ritual is not found is a tribute to Judaism which has raised marriage above these primitive ideas into something much more honourable (cf. Gen. 2. 23-5). It is, however, possible that in the Blessing of Rebekah (Gen. 24. 60) we have part of the ritual of blessing a marriage.

Nor is there any provision for special ceremonies at death. It seems probable that there were no such, the main object being the burial of the corpse as soon as possible. This lack of burial ceremony contrasts sharply with, for instance, Egyptian practice, and it is possible that we may see a connection between this and the lack of belief in an afterlife. The deceased was dead, and that was the end of the matter. There would be mourning, no doubt, and the actual burial would have a certain amount of dignity and customary ceremony, but that is rather different. So far as we know from the Old Testament, there was no special way of hallowing this occasion with religious or ritual forms.

iii. *Sacrifice*

In the sense of animal sacrifice, this is something quite remote from the practice of any of the great world-religions to-day. Our modern outlook thinks of it as something primitive and disgusting, and tends to dismiss it curtly as of little value. As Christians, we find in the New Testament the clear teaching that the entire Old Testament sacrificial system has been fulfilled, and so abrogated, by Jesus Christ: our rejection is reinforced. It is, however, well to remember that if Jesus fulfilled the sacrificial system it could only have been because it had value and significance. We must consider also that in a culture where animal sacrifice was the norm our feelings of disgust would have been absent, and those sacrificing would have seen the meaning in a different way. As students of the Old Testament, therefore, it is necessary for us to look at this institution quite dispassionately, and attempt to see its meaning and assess its significance in the same way as the men of the Old Testament.

The developed Levitical system was extremely elaborate, and for the details we must refer to the dictionaries and the specialist books. For our purpose we may distinguish three main classes of sacrifice:

(a) Sacrifices that were primarily a gift to God.

(b) Sacrifices intended primarily as a means of communion with God.

(c) Sacrifices where the main object was the release of the blood in order that atonement might be made.

It must be realized, of course, that these divisions are by no means rigid. In particular, we note that by New Testament times all sacrifices were considered to have an atoning effect. Putting it another way, whenever man comes into contact with God in the right frame of mind, there, in some way, there is reconciliation.

We also notice that not only animals were offered; so also were flour, bread, wine, oil, and incense. As a general statement, however, it may be said that these elements were offered as supplements to animal sacrifices (Num. 15; Lev.

7. 11ff), or as a parallel offering (the "shewbread", Lev. 24. 5ff) to the burnt-offering. We shall, therefore, confine our discussion to animal sacrifices.

a. *Sacrifices that were primarily a gift to God*

The clearest representative of this class is the burnt-offering (*'olah*), otherwise known as *kalil* (from "whole"). It is the name given to the offering of an animal for complete consumption by fire. Its most typical form is that for the nation as a whole, taking the form of a daily sacrifice, morning and evening (Ex. 29. 38-46. In v. 42 it is called *tamid*, "continual"), supplemented on New Moons and Sabbaths (Num. 28. 9-15) and on Festivals (Num. 28. 16—29. 39).

In origin, it was clearly intended to be food for the deity (cf. Lev. 3. 11; 22. 25), but burned, so that it could be taken up in the form of smoke (cf. Gen. 8. 21). In developed thought, of course, this idea is almost, if not entirely, absent, and the sacrifice takes the aspect of an acknowledgement of the greatness, power, and glory of God, and of thanksgiving for the mercies shown to the nation.

Although the most usual was the offering for the whole nation, burnt-offerings could also be made by individuals. It could be either as fulfilment of a promise made (e.g. Judges 11. 29ff where Jephthah offers his daughter as a burnt offering), or a freewill offering, that is, a sacrifice made in recognition of a benefit received (e.g. Gen. 8. 20, where Noah offers in thanksgiving for preservation from the Flood).

It will be clear that the motives which prompt these sacrifices are the same as those which to-day inspire the continual offering of praise and thanksgiving to God in Christian services. Such offerings, too, arise from the desires of men always to use their material goods to express their thanks to God for benefits received. From a present-day viewpoint we may think the sacrificial way crude; but looked at in terms of the culture-pattern of the Fertile Crescent it is clear and meaningful, and a good deal less barbarous than the human sacrifices which were so common a feature of worship during the pre-Exilic period, not only outside Israel, but within (cf. 2 Kings 21. 6; 23. 10, etc.).

b. *Sacrifices intended primarily as a means of communion with God*

The usual term is "peace-offering" (*shelem*), and it is disputed by scholars whether this or the "gift" sacrifice is the earlier form. In any case it is found among Semitic peoples in very primitive times, and is fundamental to any understanding of the meaning of sacrifice. The ritual is described in Lev. 3, and we have a good description of the way in which such sacrifices were carried out in historic times in 1 Sam. 1. 3-9, 21; 2. 13-16. In Lev. 7. 11ff it is anticipated that a peace-offering will be in the nature of a thanksgiving or a votive offering (i.e. in fulfilment of a vow) or a freewill offering. The payment of a vow is also mentioned in 1 Sam. 1. 21. In general these sacrifices were private offerings, the only occasions specified in the *Torah* for public peace-offerings being the consecration of a priest (Lev. 9. 4) and Pentecost (Lev. 23. 19). Records of public peace offerings are found in Josh. 8. 31; Judges 20. 26; 21. 4; 1 Sam. 11. 15; 2 Sam. 6. 17; 1 Kings 8. 63. In outline, the ritual was for the animal to be killed by the offerer; the blood was dashed on the altar, part of the animal was burned, part used for food by the priests, and the bulk used as the basis of a common meal for the offerer and those with him.

When we are assessing the origins of such rites, we need to remember that up to the Deuteronomic legislation (Deut. 12. 15ff), it was permissible to eat animal flesh only if the blood had first been offered on the altar (this rule had to be modified with the enforcement of the rule of the single sanctuary). That is, an offering of this kind was a necessary preliminary to any meat meal, as in 1 Kings 8. 63 where the enormous sacrifices listed simply mean that Solomon organized a large-scale banquet to celebrate the dedication of the Temple. Conversely, of course, every meat meal had a religious significance which is quite absent to-day.

There is, however, one great exception to the rule that peace-offerings are almost entirely private, and that is the ritual of the Passover, where the way in which the lamb is used is typical of this form of sacrifice. Strictly speaking, of course, all the lambs were private offerings, brought by the worshippers to form the basis of their own Passover suppers. The fact, however, that it was a festival of Israel as a whole, commemorating and giving thanks for national deliverance, brings it into the class of public sacrifices.

The meaning of such ceremonies is clear. The worshippers and the God are bound together by partaking in a common meal. It is a sacrifice expressing an already existing state of peace rather than one which creates peace from an existing state of disunity (for this latter the sacrifices of sin and guilt-offerings were necessary). In the Passover, it expresses Israel's acknowledgement that they are the people of God, and that each one partaking is within the Covenant and the redeemed community where he enjoys the benefits of the salvation God has wrought. In a private offering, it expresses his thankfulness for all that God has done for him, whether as payment of a vow of sacrifice if God should prosper the offerer, or as a true free-will offering.

c. *Sacrifices where the main object was the release of the blood in order that atonement might be made.*

Those in this category are particularly the guilt- and sin-offerings, and especially the great national sin-offering of the Day of Atonement. The directions are found in Lev. 4. 1—5. 13; 6. 24-30 (sin-offering), Lev. 5. 14—6. 7; 7. 1-10 (guilt-offering) and Lev. 16 (Day of Atonement). Speaking generally, the procedure is that the offerer first lays his hand on the head of the animal and then kills it. The blood is disposed of on the altar, the fat and inward parts burned, and, in the majority of cases, the rest of the animal is eaten by the priests (in one or two cases the entire carcase is burned, but not on the altar). There is a real difference between these offerings and the peace-offerings we have just discussed, in that the offerer takes no part in eating the flesh. In other words, whereas the peace-offering is witness to an already existing relationship, these are the means of making reconciliation where the relationship has been broken. There is no common meal, nor is there any element of propitiation by offering a gift (else the flesh would be burned on the altar). The propitiation comes not by making a present to an offended deity, but in the use made of the blood—a point to which we shall return shortly.

The ritual of the Day of Atonement has many points in common with this, and also a number peculiar to itself. We have already noticed that it came just before the beginning of the year, and is intended as a formal cleansing of the nation from unatoned sin. It is kept as a solemn fast by all. On that day the High Priest first makes a sin-offering for himself and his house, so that the officiating priests may be pure; but on this day only, the ceremonial manipulation of the blood takes place not on the altar but inside the Holy of Holies, on the Mercy-seat itself. Before this sacrifice is offered, two goats are brought, and chosen by lot for two rôles: one is a sin-offering for Israel, the other is "for Azazel". After his own animal has been offered the High Priest deals with the goat for the sin-offering, placing some of the blood not only on the Mercy-seat, but also on the altar to "make atonement for it". He then takes the other goat, lays his hands on its head, and confesses over it all the sins of Israel, "and he shall put them upon the head of the goat". This goat is led away into the wilderness to "bear all their iniquities upon him to a solitary land; and he shall let the goat go in the wilderness". After this, burnt-offerings are made for both High Priest and Israel as a whole, while the remains of the sin-offering animals are burned outside Jerusalem.

Although there can be no doubt that the ceremony in its present form is late, and was probably not celebrated in Jerusalem before the time of Ezra, there can also be little doubt that in many ways it goes back much further. The idea of the goat carrying away the sins of the people into the wilderness "for Azazel"—probably a wilderness evil spirit—is quite separate from the idea of sacrifice for sins, and this ceremony has the mark of something much more ancient than the Priestly Code.

Two further points stand out as needing discussion—the laying-on of hands, and the use made of the blood in atonement sacrifices generally. If we consider the laying-on of hands, it might appear that it has the same purpose as with the goat "for Azazel"— that is, the transference of the sin to the goat. A little reflection will show that this cannot be so : in the first place, the confession of sin is not mentioned in the ritual, as it surely would be if it were necessary; secondly, the goat for Azazel is not offered to God, but rather the contrary; thirdly, and most important, to pass the sin on to the animal would be clean contrary to the whole Hebrew belief that only a perfect and unblemished beast could be sacrificed. Sin would be a much greater blemish and affront to the holiness of God than any physical defect could be. Rather, we are to see it in the same light as the laying-on of hands in blessing (cf. Gen. 48. 14; Deut. 34. 9, etc.). It is not just an outward symbol, but the expression of the solemn transfer to the recipient of the power and character of the bestower in accordance with the words of blessing. In the same way, in this sacrifice the

WORSHIP, SACRIFICE, AND PRIESTHOOD   155

laying-on of hands extends the personality of the offerer into the animal, so that the presentation of its life is in effect the presentation of the life of the offerer. When this is accepted by God, reconciliation is effected.

When we consider the blood, the key text is Lev. 17. 11 :

> For the life of the flesh is in the blood; and I have given it for you upon the altar to make atonement for your souls; for it is the blood that makes atonement, by reason of the life.

We have looked at this passage briefly in considering the psychical function of blood. We need to notice that in these sacrifices the main object is not the slaying of the animal, but the release of its life for ceremonial use. In one way, we may say that the death of the animal is not essential at all, but incidental, as is shown by the fact that no use is made of the corpse. But, why use life? In the first place, life belongs to God, and must be returned to him; hence, among other things, the prohibition of the eating of blood, and the requirement that if blood is not used on the altar it is to be poured out on the ground (Deut. 12. 16; cf. Lev. 17. 13).

Secondly, we may look at the Covenant ceremony described in Exodus 24. 1-8. The essence of this ceremony is the sharing of the blood between God and the people : by sharing the one life, they are brought together in a new union. There is an analogy here with the well-known ceremony of blood brotherhood. The point to notice is that the life poured out is not dead, but still active.

Thirdly, we have already noticed that the laying-on of hands is a ceremony of identification. Since the worshipper identifies himself with the sacrificial animal, its life is, to that extent, the life of the offerer. The sin which calls for the offering is sin which demands the life of the sinner (not moral sins only, but ritual sins also, cf. 2 Sam. 6. 6, 7). We remember that it was not *any* animal which could be used for sacrifice: the classes are clearly defined, and in particular we may notice that it had to be a domesticated animal (no wild animal could be used), and to be the property of the offerer (cf. 2 Sam. 24. 24). We have noticed the way in which the personality of a man was thought to extend into his property (pp. 87-90, above), and this extension is reinforced by the laying-on of hands. In offering the animal he was, in fact, offering part of himself. The sacrifice is not of a substitute, in the sense that the animal's life is offered *instead of* the life of the offerer, but representational, the part representing the whole. A man offers the life of what is his property and is part of himself, to represent the offering of his total self which is due to the deity. It is important to remember that it is very clear Jewish teaching that sacrifices offered purely ceremonially, without the right attitude of mind, are quite worthless (cf. Isa. 1. 10-17, etc.).

We may sum up our thinking about sacrifice by relating it to the main element in Hebrew life, the Covenant. The sacrifice does three things: it acknowledges the greatness and goodness of the God who made the Covenant and keeps it; it expresses the unity of the Covenant; and when the Covenant is broken it provides the means by which the estrangement may be healed. It is within this framework that all teaching on sacrifice may be understood.

iv. *The Priesthood*

We shall consider here, briefly, the functions and the development of the priestly office in Israel. By the close of the Old Testament period, of course, the system was well ⁺ablished, with a clearly defined hierarchy and duties ⁺t entirely confined to the Temple. In New Testament ⁺re were so many priests that all were not able to ⁺ but did so by "courses" (cf. Luke 1. 5, 8). In however, their functions were wider, well Deut. 33. 8-10—to use the Urim and

WORSHIP, SACRIFICE, AND PRIESTHOOD 157

Thummim, to teach ordinances and law, and to offer sacrifice of incense and burnt-offerings. The last of these has just been discussed; what of the others?

Urim and Thummim are referred to in Ex. 28. 39; Lev. 8. 8; Num. 27. 21; 1 Sam. 28. 6; Ezra 2. 63; Neh. 7. 65. They make it clear that we are dealing with a method of discovering the divine will by means of a sacred lot, and we may see how it was used when we look at those incidents where such divination was practised, in particular those of Achan (Josh. 7. 16ff) and Jonathan (1 Sam. 14. 38ff). Of the details we are ignorant, though it is clear that it was only a means of selecting one of two alternatives. It seems not improbable that they were two stones, distinguished by colour or in some other way. An arrangement or order having been determined as meaning a specific answer, the stones were thrown, and the result taken as directions from Yahweh (cf. 1 Sam. 14. 41).[24] Such a method of choice by lot also appears in the New Testament (Acts 1. 26). It is clear that the priests were the guardians of the oracle and were its authorized manipulators. This accords well with their functions as shrine guardians, and their special relationship with the deity. It also links with their functions as judges, and it is probable that the provision for the settlement of disputed cases found in Ex. 22. 8, 9 refers to the use of the lot.

In New Testament times the function of *teaching ordinance and law* (*mishpat* and *torah*) was carried out especially by the scribes. In earlier times it was the function of the priest to expound the will of God, and through him the teachings of right and wrong in any given situation were conveyed to the people. We have noticed (p. 100, above) how these were seen in terms of custom

---

[24] It is not impossible to think of other ways in which this could have been done..

158 THE RELATIONS BETWEEN GOD AND MAN

and tradition : it was the task of the priest to give a decision on what was or was not right, and to apply custom to new situations (cf. Mal. 2. 7). So grew up a corpus of teaching not unlike the case-law with which we are familiar in England to-day. The priest thus has the character not only of a cult official but also of a judge (*shophet*), a combination of functions seen clearly in the case of Samuel (e.g. 1 Sam. 7. 15-17), and in the case of Micah's levite, who gave advice not only to the family whom he served but also to outsiders (Judges 18. 1-5), while a good example of the way in which inquiry was made is seen in Hag. 2. 11-13.

When we turn to the history of the priesthood, things are rather more complicated. In the developed Priestly Code there is a clear distinction between Priests and Levites, and a particular place of honour for the High Priest. The tribe of Levi is the priestly tribe, and only those reckoned as its members may have anything to do with the service of the sanctuary. However, not all members of the tribe are priests : that distinction is reserved for those reckoned to be descendants of Aaron, and it is one of the Aaronic priests who is consecrated as High Priest. The Priestly Code takes this distinction between orders back to the time of the Exodus, but as we shall see, it is more than doubtful if this is justified. We ought also to look a little more closely at the meaning of the words priest (*kohen*) and levite (*lewi*) before considering the history of the institutions.

Kohen probably has the basic meaning of "one who stands", e.g. as a servant, and hence the servant of God at a shrine. There may also be some connection with the meaning "soothsayer", and in later times it comes to mean "sacrificer", as opposed to other shrine servants who did not undertake this duty.

Lewi has a more complicated history. It is used in the Old Testament to signify both a member of the tribe of Levi, and also a person specially concerned with the cult.

WORSHIP, SACRIFICE, AND PRIESTHOOD   159

In later times, as we have noticed, these two meanings became merged, but there is every indication that this was not so earlier. The actual meaning of the word itself is far from clear, but it is probable that it derives from a root which in other languages has the meaning of "priest".

A most interesting passage in this connection is Judges 17. Micah the Ephraimite built himself a shrine, and installed one of his sons (also an Ephraimite, naturally) as priest. This was obviously felt to be not an ideal arrangement, for when the chance comes of having a "proper" priest, it is taken, the man installed being a levite *of the tribe of Judah*. It is evident that priestly functions were not confined to one tribe only, and the restriction of sacrifice to the Aaronic line is not yet. It looks very much as if at this time the word "levite" meant simply one who had been apprenticed to the profession, and so had at his fingertips the proper forms and rituals. This is not an isolated case. In 2 Samuel 8. 18 we learn that David's sons (Judahites) were priests: Gideon offers sacrifice (Judges 6. 25ff), as does Manoah, a Danite (Judges 13. 15ff), and Elijah (1 Kings 18. 30ff). Samuel himself was an Ephraimite by birth (1 Sam. 1. 2) though frequently represented as performing priestly functions. The implication is clear that in early days the function of priesthood was not confined to one tribe, but was legitimately exercised by men from all the tribes. It seems not impossible that the actual tribe of Levi was wiped out before or during the conquest of Canaan (Gen. 34 has been suggested in this connection), and that in later times the similarity of names led to identification of levites with the tribe of Levi.

In Deuteronomy the phrase "the priests the levites" is used (17. 9; 24. 8) while the clear implication of 33. 8-11 is that there was as yet no distinction between the two orders. When exactly the split came is not known, though we may conjecture that it was not unconnected with the reform of Josiah (2 Kings 23). At that time the local sanctuaries were closed, but their priests did not take part in the Jerusalem cultus (v. 9), which remained the province of the house of Zadok.[25] In Ezek. 44. 9ff it is specifically ordered that those who are of the houses of the priests of local shrines are to minister in the Temple, but only as attendants and not as priests. It is noteworthy that the distinction between priests and levites is found only in the Priestly Code, and therefore clearly reflects post-exilic practice.

The office of High Priest as such is not found before the Exile: as we have seen that office was in effect filled by the King. After the Exile, when there was no king, the spiritual leader of the nation also gained a good deal of secular power, and so the High Priest became the outstanding figure. In the Maccabaean period the two offices were conjoined once more, but separated again after the fall of that house. The High Priesthood in Israel came to an end with the fall of the Temple in A.D. 70. As Christians, we believe that we now have a great and permanent High Priest, who has fulfilled all the functions of priesthood, and now remains our mediator for ever, having entered once for all into the Holy Place with his own blood to make expiation for the sins of all mankind.

---

[25] It is worth noting that the Zadokites only become prominent after the capture of Jerusalem. Up till then Abiathar was David's priest. It is by no means impossible that Zadok was Jebusite priest of the Jerusalem shrine (cf. Medchi*zedek*), taken over with the city, and eventually becoming supreme after backing Solomon on the death of David (1 Kings 2. 26, 27).

EPILOGUE

The Faith of Israel is not a dead faith, enshrined in a book, a mere object of scholarly study. The Old Testament is witness to the living experience of Israel through the ages when they were growing in the knowledge of God, coming to spiritual knowledge and insight far beyond that of any other nation. The same nation, Israel, lives by the same faith to-day. Christians often suppose that the faith of the Jew is a debased faith which, now that Christ has come, has no more meaning or purpose. As Christians we may, and must, proclaim gladly that Judaism is taken up and transcended, and that we are called to a higher faith in Jesus. Yet, if we are honest, we must acknowledge that only too often our Christianity is meaningless, and that we fall back far below the level from which Christianity sprang. The Christian has both greater opportunities for life, and greater possibilities of fall. Rather, we must acknowledge Judaism as a living faith, the inspiration of millions, which has been the inspiration also of two other great world-religions,[1] and which to-day provides a knowledge of God and his ways far beyond what the majority of us have in spite of our nominal Christianity. We cannot but take the Old Testament seriously, and thank God for it. It is not only the indispensable prelude to the New Testament, the rock whence we were hewn, but a living word of God in its own right.

[1] Christianity and Islam.

EPILOGUE

It has been the object of this book to show the way in which the Jew of Old Testament times understood himself and his God. It has been our argument that in the Old Testament we have not simply the record of the evolution of religious ideas among the Hebrews, but a faith stemming direct from God's self-revelation of himself. That there is development, no one can deny. But that development is not natural evolution, nor is it what some would call "Progressive Revelation" (for such a term implies that in the early stages God deliberately withholds some part of himself). Rather, it is the way in which the Hebrews gradually came to understand more and more of what was already implicit in what God had given them in his mighty acts and in his covenant, a growth fostered by his continuing direct action through inspired leaders. God was not, through these men, revealing something new, but was making clear what they ought to have understood from what they already knew of him. The decisive events are those connected with the Exodus and the making of the Covenant, probably the most important historical complex in the whole history of mankind, since it set man's whole spiritual life on a new path, and has affected, and still affects, the whole of world history. If for that reason alone, the Faith of Israel is a worthy study for man to-day, and one which, if followed faithfully and honestly, will bring him face to face with the God who acts both in history and in the lives of men.

FOR FURTHER STUDY

Any adequate understanding of the Old Testament must be based on a sound foundation of the history. Recent histories which may be thoroughly recommended are:

> Anderson, B. W. *The Living World of the Old Testament* Longmans, 1958
>
> Bright, J. *A History of Israel* S.C.M., 1960
>
> Gottwald, N. K. *A Light to the Nations* Harper, New York, 1959

By far the most valuable way of studying the words used in the Old Testament is by use of a Bible and Concordance. The most generally useful is Young's *Analytical Concordance,* which makes it possible to distinguish different Hebrew words even though translated by the same word in English. Along with this, reference should be made to the various dictionaries, particularly valuable being:

> Von Allmen, J. J. (ed.) *Vocabulary of the Bible* Lutterworth, 1958
>
> Richardson, A. (ed.) *Theological Word Book of the Bible* S.C.M., 1950

and the articles from Kittel's *Wörterbuch* edited and translated by J. R. Coates in the *Bible Key Words* series, published by A. and C. Black.

A good summary of recent critical work on the Old Testament will be found in:

> Rowley, H. H. (ed.) *The Old Testament and Modern Study* Oxford, 1951 (cheap edition, 1961)

see also: Hahn, H. *The Old Testament and Modern Research.* S.C.M., 1956

The following books, though by no means an exhaustive list, will be found useful in following up many points made in the text:

> Bright, J. *The Kingdom of God in Bible and Church* Lutterworth, 1955
>
> Chase, M. E. *Life and Language in the Old Testament* Collins, 1956
>
> de Vaux, R. *Ancient Israel: its Life and Institutions* E. T., Darton, Longman, and Todd, 1961
>
> Gray, G. B. *Sacrifice in the Old Testament* Oxford, 1925 (now O.P.)
>
> Herbert, A. S. *Worship in Ancient Israel* Lutterworth, 1959
>
> Jacob, E. *Theology of the Old Testament* E.T., Hodder, 1958
>
> Köhler, L. *Hebrew Man* E.T., S.C.M., 1956
>
> Meek, T. J. *Hebrew Origins* Harper, New York, Revised Edition 1950
>
> Robinson, H. W. *The Religious Ideas of the Old Testament* Second Edition, Duckworth, 1956
>
> Robinson, H. W. *The Christian Doctrine of Man* T. and T. Clark, 1911
>
> Robinson, T. H. *Prophecy and the Prophets in Ancient Israel* Duckworth, 1923

Rowley, H. H. *The Rediscovery of the Old Testament* James Clarke, n.d.

Rowley, H. H. *The Faith of Israel* S.C.M., 1956

Snaith, N. H. *The Distinctive Ideas of the Old Testament* Epworth, 1944

Tennant, F. R. *The Sources of the Doctrine of the Fall and Original Sin* Cambridge, 1903 (now O.P.)

Vriezen, T. C. *An Outline of Old Testament Theology* E. T., Blackwell, 1958

Wright, G. E., and Fuller, R. H. *The Books of the Acts of God* Duckworth, 1960

(The date given refers in each case to first publication. Most have been reprinted a number of times, and are still in print.)

INDEX OF BIBLICAL REFERENCES

OLD TESTAMENT

Genesis

1. 1—2. 4a	58, 61
1. 2	128
1. 31	61
2. 1-3	141
2. 4ff	58
2. 7	78
2. 19	78
2. 23	81, 148
2. 24	9, 81, 148
2. 25	148
3	63, 70
3. 5	105
3. 22	105
4. 7	97
4. 10	82
4. 12-14	100
6. 1-7	2, 104, 106
6. 9	106
6. 12	80, 81
6. 13	81
7. 22	82n
8. 1	84
8. 20	150
8. 21	150
9. 8-17	10, 81
11. 1-9	68
14	144
15. 7-21	8, 10
16. 7-13	69

Genesis (cont.)

17. 1-22	69
17. 5-6	71
17. 9ff	147
17. 19-21	10
19	69n
21. 25-32	9
22	146, 147n
24. 60	148
28. 10-22	68, 133, 135
31. 13	137
31. 36	95
32. 22-32	71
34	159
34. 7	100
35. 4	135
35. 8	135
37. 27	81
40	114
41	114
41. 38	129
48. 14	154
49. 6	73

Exodus

3. 1—4. 17	67, 69, 125
4. 24-5	147
6. 9	85
7. 14-21	14
10. 21-9	14

INDEX OF BIBLICAL REFERENCES

Exodus (cont.)

12. 8	81
12. 11	140
12. 26-7	7
12. 48	147
13. 12ff	146
14. 5	83
15. 10	84
15. 21	7
18. 15-20	122
19. 5, 6	11, 47
19. 18	68
20. 2	5
20. 3	14
20. 5	89, 100
20. 11	58, 141
20. 22—23. 33	10, 21
20. 24	133, 134
21. 16	25
22. 8	157
22. 9	95, 157
22. 21ff	25
23. 9	25
23. 14, 15	139
24. 1-8	8, 155
24. 15-17	73, 75
25. 10	67
25. 17-22	67
28. 3	129
28. 39	157
29. 38-46	150
30. 22ff	143
31. 2-5	129
32. 11ff	125
33. 18	73
34. 6, 7	13
34. 19, 20	39, 146
34. 22	140
40. 2	141
40. 17	141

Leviticus

3	151
3. 11	150

Leviticus (cont.)

4. 1—6. 7	97, 152
4. 22	98
5. 1	98
5. 2	98
5. 2-6	98n
5. 4	98
5. 16	98
6. 24-30	152
7. 1-10	152
7. 11ff	150, 151
8. 8	159
9. 4	151
12	145
14. 33-47	99n
16	100, 153
16. 21	31
17. 11	11, 81, 155
17. 13	155
17. 14	81
19. 2	31
19. 11	31
19. 15	23, 31
22. 5-9	31
22. 25	150
23. 9ff	140
23. 19	151
24. 5ff	150
25. 25	39
26. 11	79

Numbers

3. 46ff	146
6. 1-21	115
6. 27	72
10. 10	141
10. 35, 36	66
11. 17	129
13. 33	106
14. 21-3	73
15	149
15. 28-31	96
16. 22	85
18. 15ff	146

168 INDEX OF BIBLICAL REFERENCES

Numbers (cont.)

21. 6-9	65
23. 10	78
24. 2	129
27. 18	129
27. 21	157
28. 9-15	141, 150
28. 16—29. 39	150
29. 7-11	141
35. 19ff	39
35. 31	97

Deuteronomy

4. 29	82
5.1	51
5.6	5
5. 12-15	58, 142
5. 22-4	74
6. 20-4	6
7. 6-9	1, 22
7. 9	18
9. 13, 14	112
10. 2	67
10. 12-22	147
12. 1-4	59
12. 1-14	135
12. 11	72
12. 15ff	151
12. 16	155
12. 29-31	59
13. 1-5	118
15. 9-10	83
16. 1-8	140
16. 9ff	140
17. 8-12	122
17. 9	159
17. 14-20	45
18. 9ff	59
18. 11	111
18. 20-2	116, 118
19.6	39, 83
19. 12	39
23. 17	29
24. 8	159

Deuteronomy (cont.)

24. 16	91
25. 5-10	39, 112
26. 5	92
28. 65	83
31. 21	106
33. 8-11	155, 159
34. 9	154
34. 10	125

Joshua

4. 19—5. 9	135
5. 2ff	146
5. 9	147
6. 17-19	88
7	88
7. 10-12	88
7. 16ff	157
8. 31	151
10. 40	56
13. 13	56
16. 10	56
17. 13	56
24. 26	135

Judges

1. 16	92
1. 16-36	56, 92
2. 11-19	57
3. 10	129
4. 4—5. 31	44
4. 5	135
4. 11	92
6. 7—8. 32	44
6. 11	135
6. 25ff	159
6. 34	129
9	9, 45
11. 29	129
11. 29ff	150
13	69
13. 5	115
13. 7	115

INDEX OF BIBLICAL REFERENCES

Judges (cont.)

13. 15ff	159
14. 1ff	92
15. 19	85
17	159
18. 1-5	158
18. 20	84
19. 30	100
20. 16	96
20. 26	151
21. 4	151

Ruth

3. 1—4. 6	39
3. 7	84
4. 1-13	112

1 Samuel

1. 2	159
1. 3	91
1. 3-9	151
1. 8	83
1. 15	85
1. 21	91, 151
2. 6	111
2. 13	91
2. 13-16	151
2. 22-5	25
3	125
3. 10-14	25
4. 6-7	66
4. 22	66
7. 15-17	158
8. 1-22	45
9. 1ff	114
9. 9	113
9. 15—10. 1	45
10. 5ff	114
10. 6	129
10. 17-27	45
10. 18, 19	32, 44
11	45
11. 15	151

1 Samuel (cont.)

12. 1-25	45
14. 38ff	96, 157
14. 41	157
15. 17ff	46
15. 24-6	52
16. 1ff	46
18. 1-4	8
18. 10	114
19. 18-24	114
19. 20	129
20. 5	141
20. 14-16	20
20. 24	141
21. 4-6	30
24. 11	95
26. 19	14, 90, 93, 100, 136n
26. 20	100
26. 21	96
28. 6	157
28. 7-19	110
30. 12	85

2 Samuel

2. 3, 4	46
3. 27-30	89
5. 1-3	46
6. 6-8	30, 155
6. 16	66
6. 17, 18	144, 151
7. 12-16	48
8. 18	159
11. 2—12. 25	25
11. 3ff	92
12. 1-15	115
12. 7-23	125
13. 12	100
13. 28	84
14. 5-7	89
15. 1-6	51
15. 18	92
21. 1-9	89
23. 1, 2	130
24. 24	156

INDEX OF BIBLICAL REFERENCES

1 Kings

1	46, 115
1. 32-40	119, 143
1. 39-40	46
2. 26-7	160n
3. 2, 3	135
3. 4ff	125
8	144
8. 6	67
8. 9	67
8. 10, 11	75
8. 27-30	68
8. 46	103
8. 63	151, 152
8. 66	84
11. 1ff	57, 92
11. 29	119
11. 29-40	46, 115
12	9, 46
12. 19	94
12. 28-30	65n
14. 2	119
17. 1	125
18. 20-9	114
18. 30ff	159
18. 46	115
19. 1-18	67
19. 2	26
19. 4	125
19. 9ff	125
20. 26-34	8
21	25
21. 3	112
22	118
22. 5ff	115

2 Kings

1. 1	94
2. 3	115, 121
2. 9ff	115, 121
2. 15	85
3. 5	94
3. 7	94
3. 15	115

2 Kings (cont.)

4. 23	142
5. 17	14, 15, 67, 93, 136n
5. 19-27	99
5. 27	89
6. 15ff	115
9	46, 115
11. 4-16	142
11. 11, 12	143
11. 17	46
15. 1-7	144
16. 10ff	59
18. 1-5	59, 66
21. 6	151
23	59, 135, 160
23. 1-3	9
23. 7	29
23. 9	160
23. 10	151
23. 21-3	140
23. 37	60

1 Chronicles

29. 18, 19	83

2 Chronicles

23.3	9
26. 16ff	144
36. 22	85

Ezra

1. 5	85
2. 63	157
9. 5ff	126
9. 9	19

Nehemiah

7. 65	157
9. 6ff	126

Esther

4. 13	79

# INDEX OF BIBLICAL REFERENCES

Job	
4. 7-11	102
4. 9	84
5. 24	96
6. 28-30	102
8. 3-7	102
11. 13-20	102
14. 20-2	109
17. 1	85
17. 13	109
19. 25	40
27. 6	83
30. 25	79
31	102
32. 8	129
33. 4	129
34. 36, 37	95
38—41	60, 63

Psalms	
1	102
2	143
6. 4, 5	19, 110
7. 9	86
8	60
8. 3-8	63, 107
10. 12	27
10. 14	27
12. 5	27
16. 9, 10	80
19	60, 63
21	143
22	127
23. 2, 3	24
29. 1-3	73
29. 5-9	73
30. 4	20
31. 24	83
32. 6	20
33	60, 64
33. 6	64, 128
37. 22	102
37. 25	102
42	127
42. 3ff	93

Psalms (cont.)	
43	127
45	145
49. 14, 15	111
50	120
51	127
51. 1	19
51. 5	104
51. 6-12	100, 131
51. 10, 11	130
56. 4	80
57. 7, 8	72
58. 3	104
62. 9	72
72	143
73	102, 127
73. 12-20	99, 102
73. 24	111
78. 17, 18	83
80. 1	67
81	120
81. 3, 4	141
81. 4-7	7
81. 10	7
84. 2	81
85. 9, 10	74
93	47
95	47, 60, 120
96	47
96. 10	51
97	47, 73
98	47
99	47
99. 1	67
101. 5	83
104	60
104. 14, 15	83
104. 30	128
106. 7-11	6
109. 13	112
109. 16	20
110	143
112. 9	72
119	28, 122
119. 124	19

INDEX OF BIBLICAL REFERENCES

Psalms (cont.)

132. 5	68
132. 11, 12	48
132. 13	68
135. 17	84
135. 21	68
136	60
137	136
139. 7, 8	110, 131
143. 2	103
143. 10	130, 131
148	60

Proverbs

1. 8	122
3. 1	122
3. 11, 12	22
4. 2	122
6. 22, 23	122
8. 1-31	60, 64
11. 17	20
14. 29	85
19. 2	96
20. 6	19
20. 9	103

Ecclesiastes

6. 2	79
7. 20	103
9. 5, 6	109

Isaiah

1. 2	95
1. 10-17	156
1. 11-15	119
1. 12, 13	31
1. 13, 14	141
1. 15-17	31
1. 27, 28	52
4. 2-4	34
5. 16	30
6. 1-7	65, 120, 125, 144
6. 3	29, 74
6. 5	29, 104

Isaiah (cont.)

7. 10ff	125
7. 14	35
8. 11ff	125
8. 19	111
9. 2-7	35
10. 5, 6	16
10. 5-19	54
10.12	16
10. 20-2	34
10. 24-7	54
11. 1ff	35, 131
11. 2	129
11. 6-9	62
11. 11	34
11. 16	34
14. 5	110
14. 9-11	110
26. 3	106
26. 9	85
26. 19	111
30. 1-5	15
30. 10	118
31. 3	80
32. 1-8	35
34. 16	131
38. 18	110
40. 1, 2	38
40. 6	18
40. 10, 11	38
40. 22, 23	17
41. 8	41
41. 14	38
42. 1	130
42. 1-4	41, 51
42. 5	85
42. 5-9	41
42. 6, 7	17
42. 24, 25	28
43. 1	28
43. 3	40
43. 16	4
44. 1	41
44. 6	13
45. 1	17

INDEX OF BIBLICAL REFERENCES

Isaiah (cont.)

45. 1-7	54
45. 4, 5	17
45. 21-5	32, 38, 40
46. 3, 4	38
48. 8	104
48. 16	131
49. 1-6	41
49. 4	41
49. 6	40
50. 4-9	41
51. 7	122
51. 9-11	5
52. 13—53. 12	41
52. 15	42
55. 2, 3	19
58. 2	51
58. 13, 14	142
60. 1-3	74
60. 3	43
60. 10-16	43
61. 1ff	43, 131
61. 5, 6	43
61. 10	79
63. 7ff	131
63. 9	23
66. 22	112
66. 23	81

Jeremiah

1. 1	119
1. 13-16	54
1. 15	16
2. 5, 6	4
4. 19-21	116
5. 4, 5	50
5. 31	118
6. 8	79
7. 2ff	120
11. 9-11	52
11. 20	86
11. 21	116
12. 1ff	90, 124
12. 2	86
14. 15ff	118

Jeremiah (cont.)

19. 14ff	120
20. 7ff	90, 124
23. 5, 6	48
23. 7, 8	5
23. 9	116
23. 9-32	118
24. 1	120
26. 2	120
26. 4, 5	122
27	118
28	118
28. 9	116
29. 10-14	54
31. 2, 3	22
31. 31-4	11, 37
32. 1-5	54
34. 18, 19	8
35. 5-10	115
36	121
36. 5	90, 120
36. 6	120
44. 15ff	60
48. 13	137
51. 11	85

Lamentations

4. 20	84

Ezekiel

1. 3	119
1. 26	71
1. 28	71
2	126
3	126
3. 26	116
4. 4-8	116
6. 3, 4	135
6. 11	116
8	60
11. 1	130
11. 17-19	36
11. 19, 20	80

INDEX OF BIBLICAL REFERENCES

Ezekiel (cont.)

13	136
13. 3	85
16. 3	92
18	91
18. 28	95
20. 45-7	116
23. 2-4	4
33. 31	86
34. 11-16	37
34. 22-4	49
36. 27	130
37. 1-14	37, 130
43. 1-4	71
44. 9ff	160
45. 10	23

Daniel

4	114
6. 10	126
7. 22	52
11. 25	84
12. 2	111

Hosea

2. 1-17	59
2. 5	33
2. 8	55
2. 9-13	33
2. 14, 15	33
2. 19, 20	33
3. 1	21
4. 13-19	135
6. 1-3	120
6. 6	20, 119
9. 7	115
9. 15	22
11. 1	4, 22
11. 5, 6	26
11. 8, 9	26
13. 4	4
13. 14	111

Joel

2. 28ff	114, 131

Amos

1. 1—2. 3	16
1. 2	68
2. 6	24, 25
2. 7	24
2. 9-16	25
2. 11	115
2. 12	24, 115
3. 1	4, 25
3. 2	23, 25
3. 8	125
4. 1	25
4. 4, 5	26, 119
4. 13	59, 121
5. 7	24
5. 8, 9	59, 121
5. 12	24, 95
5. 18-20	33
5. 21-4	25
5. 24	24
5. 25, 26	25
5. 27	26
6. 4-6	25
7. 9	26
7. 12	113
7. 14	115
7. 15	125
8. 4-6	25
8. 5	141, 142
9. 5, 6	121
9. 7	16, 54

Jonah

4. 1ff	126

Micah

3. 5	117
3. 7	113
3. 8	129
3. 11	118
5. 13, 14	135
6. 7	80
7. 15	5
7. 16-20	121

INDEX OF BIBLICAL REFERENCES 175

Nahum		Zechariah	
2. 13—3. 4	54	7. 12	122
		8. 3	68
Habakkuk		8. 22, 23	43
1. 13	86	12. 7-14	49
		12. 10	131
Haggai		13. 1	49
1. 14	85		
2. 4, 5	131	Malachi	
2. 11-13	158	2. 7	158
		2. 14	8

APOCRYPHA

Wisdom		Prayer of Manasses	126
2. 23, 24	106		
7. 22ff	130	1 Maccabees	
9. 17	130	2. 42	20
		4. 52-9	139
Ecclesiasticus			
17. 1-14	10		
25. 24	106	2 Maccabees	
50. 5ff	141	10. 1-8	139

NEW TESTAMENT

Matthew		John	
10. 17	138	4. 9	137
22. 23ff	39	4. 20	137
23	100	10. 22	139
Mark		Acts	
7. 1ff	123	1. 26	157
11. 15ff	138	2. 30, 31	49
		6. 9	138
Luke		23. 8	108
1. 5	156		
1. 8	156	Romans	
1. 59	147	1. 20	64
2. 41, 42	147	7. 7ff	105
4. 16ff	131	7. 14	80
20. 27	108	8. 21, 22	62

INDEX OF BIBLICAL REFERENCES

1 Corinthians
15. 19   109

Galations
5. 16-24   80

Hebrews
9. 4   67n